CALIFORNIA WILDLIFE

RECORD BOOK

FIRST EDITION

2002

I

Published By

CALIFORNIA DEER ASSOCIATION BOARD OF DIRECTORS
820 PARK ROW, PMB 671
SALINAS, CA 93901-2406

California Wildlife Record Book
This Publication is Limited
0400 of 1525
First Edition, 2002

Library of Congress Control Number 2002107081
ISBN 0-9721853-0-5

CALIFORNIA DEER ASSOCIATION
CALIFORNIA STATE RECORD BOOK

FOREWORD TO THE
FIRST EDITION OF THE
CALIFORNIA WILDLIFE RECORD BOOK

California, in the world of hunting, is virtually an unknown state. The California Deer Association has put together the first conclusive, definitive record book for the state. The longest trip begins with the first step, and the tabulations are the first step of recognition for the many superb animals this state has produced.

This record book will deal with only the native, non-introduced big game animals if California and shall use the respected Boone & Crockett Club scoring system. This has been the universally accepted method of evaluation trophies of big game for over 50 years.

The categories that will be covered are deer, elk, bear, sheep, and antelope. Mountain lion will not be covered because there has never been a single lion that made the B&C minimum and the current prohibition against hunting them. One may not even possess part of one unless a special permit is had.

When the National Collection of Heads and Horns was unveiled to the public in 1991 in Cody Wyoming, after 50 years of being hidden, it was the greatest on going display of Northern American Big Game ever assembled. There are several specimens that have been displayed in it, just from California.

Just north of Los Angeles is a stretch of road called the "grapevine." Drivers are so busy speeding by to and from LA, that they don't realize this is the home of the #3 Black Bear in the B&C records. Large bears also come from Tulare, Kern, and other counties of the state. Bears are entered on the basis of skull measurement only, not by weight nor hide size.

Mule Deer will be divided into two categories, typical and non-typical. The non-typical buck that appeared for many years on the cover of the B&C scoring manual is the Harold Laird buck from Mariposa Co. scoring 319 4/8 pts. The 1st Place non-typical Award in 1989 went to Artie McGram's buck from Burney that scored 305 6/8 pts. A few typical bucks have made it and California has the ability in the past to produce bucks of unusual size.

Blacktails are the major deer that cover the coastal areas and have the most divergent habitat types. Far more California Blacktails are in the book from California than from any of their other states. The former state record, the Peter Gerbo head (scoring 166 2/8 pts), opened the Head and Horns Collection in 1991. Many fine Blacktails are out there every year and they are pursed by a very ardent fraternity.

From the 1890's, there were too few sheep in the deserts and mountains of California to permit any hunting at all. There were several "pick ups" that were located of tremendous size, but no hunting was allowed. In the mid 1890's, due to herd management and conservation, hunting in limited numbers was allowed after nearly a century of closure. California has both the desert sheep and the California Bighorn (a sub species of the Rocky Mountain Bighorn). Only the records for the desert sheep will be shown as there is not yet any season on the California Bighorn.

The arid areas of California provide some perfect areas for antelope throughout the state. In the 1850's, they were found in some of the coastal valleys near Salinas as well as many of the arid open areas of the state that had grasses and sage. But the 1849 gold rush eliminated a lot of their numbers as the demand for the meat by the miners always remained high and later habitat was lost to agriculture. Today there are several herds throughout the state that are producing top scoring heads that rank near the top. The odds of taking a top scoring head are better in California than most other states when the numbers are seen. Although small, these speed goats of the plains can provide a worthwhile challenge.

California is the ONLY state to have all 3 different types of elk within its boundaries. The Roosevelt occupy the heavy rain forests along the northern coast and other small pockets. Many live on private timber company lands and have found that niche to grow to extreme size and proportions for Roosevelt elk.

The Rocky Mountain elk are present in a couple of areas and a huntable population is thriving around Shasta Lake to the north. There is limited hunting of this group, and only one to date has met the B&C minimum scoring for Rocky Mountain elk.

The Tule elk is found only in California and in the 1840's numbered over 500,000. Then came the gold rush and the market hunters decimated them for the meat needs of the miners and cities. When things settled down, there were 2 bulls and six cows between them and extinction. Those remaining elk were taken to the Miller-Lux ranch and the uphill road of propagation began and small herds were transplanted. In that same time frame, much of their habitat was transformed into farm land and large cattle holdings. Several of the transplant herds did not make it and in the 1970's the concept of satellite herds were implemented. Now there are in excess of 28 herds, numbering over 3,500 animals roaming the state... on less than 1% of their original range. The largest known wild Tule elk gross scored 425 pts and netted 403 pts (Roosevelt elk method) and drowned off Grizzly Island in 1995. Today, there are numerous hunts one can apply for as well as land owner tags tags. The Tule elk is the greatest conservation story of the 20th century... 8 from extinction to a viable hunting population... that the sportsman and landowners can take credit for.

This tabulation of the records of California is the first step in creating a repository of hunting knowledge for the future. It is not said to be totally complete, as there are many heads out there that haven't been entered or even known about. All CDA members are encouraged to try and locate these heads so they have their place in California history.

As for a source of where one can plan a hunt for a wall hanger, or locate where the big ones have come from in the past, this will be the source of that information. Hunters can take pride in their accomplishments when their names appear with their trophy animal.

When it comes out, it will certainly be a collector's item, due to limited numbers of the first edition. They make wonderful gifts and can be responsible for many hours of fireside enjoyment in seeing the fine animals the state has produced.

Help CDA make this book all it can be by searching out potential entries and getting them in.

September 2000
James McBride, Glen Ellen, California

CONTENTS

THE CALIFORNIA WILDLIFE RECORD PROGRAM

The California Deer Association has established the California Wildlife Records Book for ongoing record keeping of wildlife species native and introduced to the state of California. Our objectives for this program are:

1. Introduce and promote hunting in its most ethical form for families as well as individuals for all to enjoy for future generations.

2. Maintain an ongoing records keeping program for outstanding trophies taken in the state of California

3. Establish a code of ethics among hunters in the strictest form of fair chase.

Recognition Awards

The California Wildlife Record Book will be establishing annual or bi-annual big game awards program in conjunction with one of the California Deer Association's Banquets. The program will consist of entries of all big game species listed; Blacktail Deer, Mule Deer Typical, Mule Deer Non-typical, Rocky Mountain Elk, Tule Elk, Roosevelt Elk, Pronghorn Antelope, Desert Big Horn Sheep and Black Bear.

The top three animals for each category will be invited to the awards program. In addition to the top three places an honorable mention award may be given for trophies that exceed the minimum score and exhibit qualities of symmetry and are taken under extreme conditions of fair chase.

All accepted entries into the record book will receive a big game certificate verifying it's been recorded.

Another certificate will be awarded to the top three places in each category at our awards program banquet.

Big game trophies entered into the awards program must meet the following requirement:

1. The trophy must have been taken in the state of California.

2. The trophy must have been legally taken as prescribed by the rules and regulations of the California Department of Fish and Game and in accordance with fair chase standards.

3. The trophy must have been taken in the respective hunting season for the year's competition. The deadline for receipt of entries has been established as March 31 of each year.

4. First, second and third place awards will be given only to the hunters who actually harvested the trophy and meet all other requirements.

5. Honorable mention or certificate of merit awards may be issued as the committee deems appropriate.

6. The committee reserves the right to re-examine and re-measure the trophy at their discretion and specifically reserves the right to disqualify and measurements that is inaccurate. Disqualification can be made when the trophy is not made available for re-examination.

7. Approved trophies that meet the listed requirements are entered into the records program and placed into their appropriate category. The committee may decline to give an annual competition award if the trophy head or if there is not enough competition that year in a given category.

Annual or Bi-annual awards competition will be held in conjunction with one of the California Deer Association Banquets. Special tables will be arranged for the persons invited to the awards program.

All Trophies will be re-measured by the awards committee prior the the competition. Location and date for this re-measuring will be given prior to the awards competition.

The Scoring System

The California Wildlife Record Book Committee adopted the official scoring system developed by the Boone & Crockett Club. The California Wildlife Record Book Committee thanks the Boone & Crockett Club for granting permission to use their system in the scoring of big game trophies for ours records program in California.

The Boone & Crockett scoring system measures antlers and horns to the nearest 1/8 inch. In bears, the skull is measured to the nearest 1/16 inch. Antlered and horned animals are measured for symmetry between the right and left antler or horn and the differences are recorded and deducted from the total score. Each point is equivalent to one inch of horn, antler, or skull growth thus totaling an entire score for each species.

Mule Deer non-typical antlers are measured the same as a typical. Additional non-typical points are added to the total score after deductions of the typical frame have been recorded.

To date, the Boone & Crockett Club has no entry for non-typical Blacktail Deer. The California Wildlife Record Book Committee has felt compelled to form a new category for this species, since many non-typical Blacktail have been taken without recognition.

Unlike non-typical Mule Deer, Blacktail non-typicals, in most cases, lack uniform four point configuration and symmetry, thus making this trophy unique. The committee has agreed to gross score non-typical Blacktail taking no deductions, creating a score that benefits the antlers.

The California Wildlife Record Book will also include a forked horn category for Blacktail Deer since a large number of bucks sport this antler configuration, therefor should be recognized.

Old Blacktail hunters, throughout the history of California have always spoken of the "Pacific Buck", Larger in body weight than the normal Blacktail Deer, maintaining a rack that is always a forked horn, without the presence of eye guards or the G-1 measurement. These bucks tend to carry more mass in circumference than normal forked horns and tend to be higher than wide. The California Wildlife Record Book will classify these

Blacktail into their own category as "Pacific Bucks".

A southern zone for Blacktail Deer is included in the California Wildlife Record Book. This area consists of Merced, San Benito, Monterey and San Luis Obispo counties. These deer must be harvested within the A zone tag allocation, west of Interstate 5.

Boone & Crockett does not recognize these deer as Blacktail and are not included in their records keeping program. The California Wildlife Record Book will include these Blacktail Deer solely in our records keeping program, thus worded so, as not to infringe on the Boone & Crockett Clubs Blacktail Deer boundaries as described in their records keeping program.

MINIMUM SCORES

TROPHY CATEGORY	CALIFORNIA RECORD BOOK	BOONE AND CROCKETT
BLACKTAIL DEER TYPICAL	120	135
BLACKTAIL DEER NON TYPICAL	140	NO CATEGORY
BLACKTAIL DEER PACIFIC FORK	100	NO CATEGORY
BLACKTAIL DEER FORKED HORN	105	NO CATEGORY
MULE DEER TYPICAL	160	190
MULE DEER NON TYPICAL	180	230
TULE ELK	260	285
ROOSEVELT ELK	270	290
ROCKY MOUNTAIN ELK	345	375
BLACK BEAR	19	21
PRONGHORN ANTELOPE	76	82
DESERT BIGHORN SHEEP	160	168

How to Enter A Trophy

All game taken legally from California can be entered into the California Wildlife Record Book, as long as it meets minimum score requirements for its category. A 60 day drying period must follow after the animal has been taken before it can be scored.

Trophies can be submitted for scoring to an official California Wildlife Record Book scorer or any Boone & Crockett scorer. Official scorers will be listed in this chapter along with people to contact about scorers near your location.

Trophies submitted with a broken skull plates, fixed or broken antlers will be ineligible for scoring. Some exceptions will be made if accurate inside spread measurement can be obtained. This is solely at the discretion of the Record Book Committee.

Trophies that have been found dead or acquired by other hunters may be submitted for entry into the record book.

California Wildlife Record Book
Official Scorers

James "J.J." McBride
Glenn Ellen, California
(707) 935-0125

James Tonkin
Morgan Hill, California
(408) 779-4944

More scorers for the California Wildlife Record Book will be included in the 2002. After a scoring seminar is scheduled to qualify people for this purpose.

Boone & Crockett scorers can also be used to score trophy heads. A list of Boone & Crockett scorers can be obtained by contacting the California Wildlife Record Book Official measurements.

FAIR CHASE STATEMENT FOR ALL HUNTER-TAKEN TROPHIES

Fair chase, as defined by the Boone & Crockett Club, is the ethical, sportsman-like and lawful pursuit and taking of any free-ranging wild game animal in a manner that does not give the hunter an improper or unfair advantage over such game animals.

Use of any of the following methods in the taking of game shall be deemed UNFAIR CHASE and unsportsmanlike:

I. Spotting or herding game from the air, following by landing in its vicinity for the purpose of pursuit and shooting;

II. Herding, pursuing, or shooting game from any motorboat or motor vehicle;

III. Use of electronic devices for attracting, locating, or observing game, or for guiding the hunter to such game;

IV. Hunting game confined by artificial barriers, including escape-proof fenced enclosures, or hunting game transplanted solely for the purpose of commercial shooting;

V. Taking of game in a manner not in full compliance with the game laws or regulations of the federal government or of any state, province, territory, or tribal council on reservations or tribal lands;

VI. Or as may otherwise be deemed unfair or unsportsmanlike by the Executive Committee of the Boone & Crockett Club.

I certify that the trophy scored on this chart was taken in FAIR CHASE as defined above by the Boone & Crockett Club. In signing this statement, I understand that if this entry is found to be fraudulent, it will not be accepted into the Awards program and all of my prior entries are subject to deletion from future editions of Records of the North American Big Game and future entries may not be accepted.

Date: _____ Signature of Hunter: _____

(Have signature notarized by a Notary Public)

Deer Distribution in California

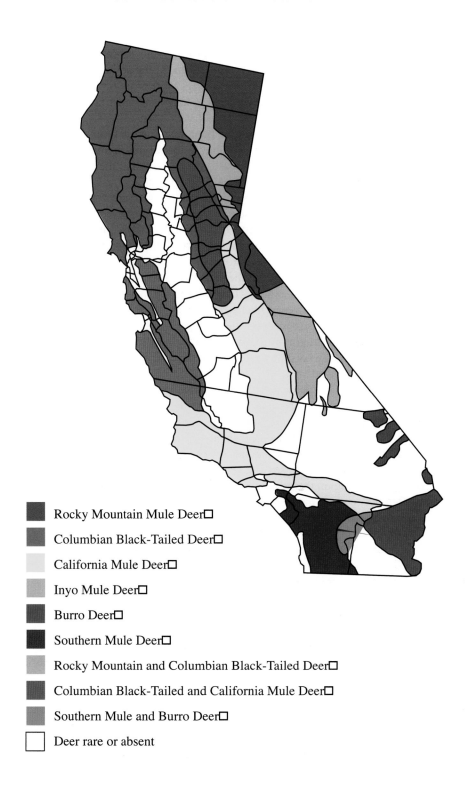

Rocky Mountain Mule Deer☐

Columbian Black-Tailed Deer☐

California Mule Deer☐

Inyo Mule Deer☐

Burro Deer☐

Southern Mule Deer☐

Rocky Mountain and Columbian Black-Tailed Deer☐

Columbian Black-Tailed and California Mule Deer☐

Southern Mule and Burro Deer☐

Deer rare or absent

The Deer of California

Written by: John Higley

WHEN MOST hunters discuss the deer they hunt they normally talk about mule deer or blacktails without any elaboration except, perhaps, for noting the size of the last buck they killed or failed to get. That's not surprising. Most of us simply do not have the expertise of a big game biologist nor do we need to know the most minute details about the deer we encounter.

On the other hand, it's a good idea for hunters to have a basic understanding of the deer in California. While you may not be able to identify each and every subspecies (there is some overlap in several areas), at least you'll know that there are recognizable differences in the deer that reside in the various geographical regions.

According to the DFG, six subspecies of mule deer are found in California: Columbian black-tailed deer (Odocoileus hemions columbiannus), Rocky Mountain mule deer (O.h. hemionus), California mule deer (O.h. californus), Inyo mule deer (O.h. inyoenis), burro mule deer (O.h. eremicus), and southern mule deer (O.h. fuliginatus).

Deer if one sort or another occupy roughly 88,000 square miles of habitat or 56 percent of the land in California. Some of the state's deer herds are resident animals that spend their entire lives in a particular area where everything they need in the way of food, cover, and water is available all year. Other herds are migratory. That is, they range high into the mountains during the summer and migrate down to winter range in the fall.

Summer range for migratory deer is usually high in elevation (from 5,000 to 10,000 feet), under public ownership, and is typically vast. By contrast, lower-elevation winter range, some public and some private, is more limited in scope and more susceptible to the type of alterations (particularly human development) that may make it unsuitable for deer. Simply put, the amount and quality of winter range generally determines the size, health, and future of many of the state's deer herds.

It is interesting how much the basic habits of deer in California differ from region to region from the type of preferred habitat to the general herd movements within that habitat. Additionally, the breeding season, or rut, occurs at slightly different times from north to south. Depending on the geographical area involved, the rut may take place anywhere from October (coastal mountains) through January (southern deserts). The factors are all taken into consideration, along with several other factors, when seasons and quotas are set by the Fish and Game Commission.

The most numerous deer in California are COLUMBIAN BLACK-TAILED DEER. They range throughout the coastal mountains from Oregon roughly to Santa Barbara, and along the west slope if the Cascade-Sierra Nevada range to Calaveras County, and south along the foothills of the Sierra Nevada to Mariposa County.

The second most abundant subspecies of deer in the state is the CALIFORNIA MULE DEER. They are found along the west slope of the Sierra Nevada from the Sierra County south into Kern County and from northern Orange County to San Benito and Monterey Counties. California mule deer also are found in the Tehachapi, San Gabriel and San Bernardino mountains.

ROCKY MOUNTAIN MULE DEER are the largest deer in California and the third most abundant subspecies. Rocky Mountain mule deer range throughout the West and spill over into the Golden State in Modoc, Lassen, Shasta and Siskiyou counties. They are also found along the east slope of the Cascade-Sierra Nevada chain to southern Mono County. Some Rocky Mountain mule deer were transplanted from Modoc County to parts of the desert mountains in San Bernardino County in 1948, where they still eke out an existence today.

SOUTHERN MULE DEER occupy portions of San Diego, Orange and western Riverside counties while the INYO MULE DEER (which may soon be classified differently based on new information) reside in Inyo, southern Mono and northern Kern counties.

BURRO MULE DEER (which have been combined with the desert mule deer, (O.h. crooki) inhabit the southeastern deserts in San Bernardino, Riverside and Imperial counties, especially along the California and Arizona sides of the Colorado River.

At the risk of confusion, it should be noted that the deer themselves have trouble recognizing one another, or perhaps they don't care. Except for the desert areas, ranges often overlap and where they do it is inevitable that the various subspecies will interbreed. Thus, the buck of your dream may very well be a hybrid.

As a general rule, adult Rocky Mountain mule deer have the largest antlers and weigh the most of the six species. There are exceptions, but characteristically pure strain black-tailed deer are the smallest of the various subspecies in California. While the die is cast genetically as to an individual animal's features, ultimately its body and antler size, and growth rate (within the framework of a particular subspecies) are determined by the quality of the habitat in which it lives. Studies (including a recent study of captive deer) have shown that deer that do not have a nutritious food supply will not develop on par with deer that have access to optimum high quality forage.

OTHER DEER? You may have heard some hunters talk about of hunting blue deer or red deer as if they're unique subspecies but that is not the case. What these hunters are seeing are deer before and after they shed their summer and winter coats (or pelage). In the summer, mule deer are reddish-brown and black-tailed deer are even a bit redder. By contrast, a mule deer's winter coat is grayish-brown while a black-tailed deer's coat varies from warm brown to gray-brown. It's reasonable to assume that a gray-brown deer could appear to have a hint of blue (to some folks) given the right conditions-thus the term blue deer comes into play.

One more thing. Contrary to what you might have read or heard, there are no free-roaming white-tailed deer (Odocoileus virginianus) in California, which isn't to say that there never have been. DFG record show that in the past there have been occasional sightings of white-tails in the northeast portion of the state. They have never become established here, however, and the last confirmed sighting was more than 50 years ago. So, while there are some white-tailed deer in portions of Oregon, Washington, Idaho, and several other western states, you won't find them in the Golden State.

CALIFORNIA'S DEER POPULATION: In the 2000 Environmental Document on Deer Hunting, the DFG estimates that the total population of deer in California is more than 511,000 animals. That is fewer deer than were estimated to be present in the 1950s, perhaps, but probably more than there were prior to the mid-1800s.

The California Gold Rush of 1849 marked the beginning of a dramatic change in California. According to one study, the greatest initial effect on deer was from market hunting to supply venison for mining camps. In 1852, it was said that there were human occupants on every gravel bar of the Trinity River from Salyer to Carville. Similar congregations were present in the Mother Lode region and even on the east slope of the Sierra Nevada.

Miners shot deer for meat year-round and deer range was altered by logging, grazing, burning and clearing. Some of the changes ultimately benefited the deer but the initial impacts caused a decline in overall numbers.

Historic game laws, hunting license requirements, and restrictions on hunting contributed to the increase of deer first noted between 1910 and 1920. In effect, legislation and enforcement allowed the deer to benefit from the improved habitat created by the intrusion of man, including the large-scale burning and logging mentioned above. More recently, however, improved fire suppression techniques have reduced the amount of deer habitat that had previously been open. At the same time, human activity has usurped prime deer habitat for agriculture uses, subdivisions, freeways, reservoirs and shopping centers.

In addition to habitat that is lost permanently, or at least for the foreseeable future, there are various other things that affect deer herds on a more immediate basis. Disturbances such as fires can actually renew some deer habitat despite their conflicts with other land uses. Prescribed burns, set deliberately in certain areas to improve habitat on small tracts of land, can also be beneficial. Old browse (brush) supports far fewer deer than new young browse, which is much more nutritious.

Meanwhile, weather variations can help or hurt deer herds depending in severity and duration. A prolonged drought, for instance, can eliminate vital water sources and stress browse plants on both summer and winter ranges. Harsh winter weather can keep deer from their winter food supply on some areas and cause a die-off to occur due to starvation. Numerous other factors take a toll on deer herds including predators, poaching, highway mortality, overgrazing by livestock and deer and disease.

Through it all, however, habitat is the key to the long-term health of deer herds. Natural causes of mortality have always been a part of the overall picture wherever big game such as deer are found. Animal population can adjust accordingly, providing the critical habitat they need still exists.

Although there have certainly been many changes in the overall landscape of California, especially during the last 150 years, there are still plenty of surprisingly good deer hunting opportunities, both on public and private land. Somewhere between the southern desert region and the Oregon border there's bound to be a deer hunting situation that will appeal to you.

DEER OF CALIFORNIA

Written by Jon Higley

(Historical Perspective of Deer in the Golden State)

EARLY EUROPEAN settlers found fewer deer in California than we have today. Things began to change rapidly in favor of deer about the time of the Gold Rush in the mid-1800s. As settlers rushed to California, heavy timber harvesting, slash fires, and wild-fires opened the forests and created vast areas where young shrubs flourished. The stage was set for deer populations to increase.

However, while the habitat was rapidly improving, unregulated killing of deer for meat and hides prevented herds from filling the newly created habitats. Many settlers, particularly miners, abandoned their diggings in favor of the more lucrative market hunting and commercial deer hunting camps that were operated throughout California from 180 until the early 1900s. One writer reported that 35,000 deer hides were shipped by a single firm in Redding in 1880.

Meanwhile, the habitat was there waiting for the deer to respond and population increases were forthcoming. In 1893, the deer season was reduced to six weeks and, in 1901, a limit of three bucks was in place. The limit was reduced to two bucks in 1905. A hunting license was required in 1907 and the revenue was used to employ wardens to enforce the regulation. Around 1910, a perfect time to be a deer, the population eruption began.

By the late 1940s, the state's deer population had increased from less than 300,000 to more than a million. Biologists began to report widespread evidence if over-population including winter losses, damage to food plants, and a reduction in fawns. In 1956, in a effort to reduce deer herds, hunters were allowed to take one deer of either sex during the last days of the season in 35 counties. The statewide harvest that year was approximately 108,000 deer which 38,000 were does.

Interestingly, the large deer kill in 1956 was followed by a significant increase in fawns. This response was expected because of notable doe harvest removed excess deer that the habitat couldn't support. The does remaining after the hunt produced more fawns because of less competition for forage. The large fawn-crops of 1957 resulted in more 2-year-old bucks in 1959. That led to record buck-harvests then and in 1960, in spite of concern by some that the herds had been decimated in 1956.

Because of public opposition to the antlerless deer harvest in 1956, legislation was passed giving 37 county boards of supervisors the authority to veto subsequent doe hunts. Today California has the dubious distinction of being the only state in the nation where doe hunts cannot always be carried out even when such hunts are biologically justified.

California deer, along with herds in most other western states, began to decline in the early 1960s. Biologists had predicted the downward trend in the 1940s because of severe damage to forage plants due to overpopulation of deer and the maturing of the habitat.

While much debate has gone on about the causes, considerable evidence exists to indicate that deer habitat quality is still in a steady decline due primarily to the loss of forage plants that grow in the wake of fires or logging. Fire and logging clear the forest of mature vegetation and allow the regrowth of shrubs and herbaceous plants that deer need for forage. In other words, a significant reduction in wildfires due to modern fire suppression capabilities and changes in forest practices designed to control brush, have resulted in loses of deer habitat. Ultimately, deer numbers are determined by the amount of good habitat available to them.

Good habitat consists of three components: food, cover and water. Each of these elements is important but research shows that food quality and quantity usually limit deer numbers even when the other components are adequate. Deer are primarily browsers and their most important food consists of young shrubs. Not surprisingly, some brush species are much more important than others. For example, manzanita, a plant that most hunters are familiar with, supplies cover but has very little forage value for deer. On the other hand, shrubs in the rose family, known as Ceanothus, are very important and of high value. In the drier, eastern areas of California, bitterbrush is a major component in the diet of mule deer.

Deer also depend on herbaceous or "weedy" plants such as clovers, particularly during the spring and summer months. In the fall, acorns are also important to them in many parts of the state.

Prime forage is not only palatable for deer but nutritious as well. Good food produces energy and contributes bone and tissue for growth and reproduction. Studies have shown that for optimum growth, deer require a diet with at least 16 percent digestible protein and preferable 20 percent during their early, rapid growth years. According to surveys, many of the plants on California deer ranges provide only 10 percent protein. Deer on such low-protein diets may only obtain 60 or 70 percent of their potential growth. In a poor forage situation, undernourished deer typically have fewer fawns and the overall population declines.

Habitats are said to have a carrying capacity. If the habitat is good and the deer are below the carrying capacity, the deer will produce more fawns thus filling the capacity. When the habitat declines for one reason or another, deer numbers also drop.

When deer numbers are low, hunters often suggest restricting hunting seasons and bag limits, or call for predator control to let the herds build up. While these suggestions are well intentioned, they do not take into account the intricate balance between deaths, births and carrying capacity. It is this balance between births and deaths that usually create the controversy over how most cases if deaths are reduced by hunting or reducing predators, the herd balances itself through increased adult loses via factors such as starvation, disease and declining births.

Efforts to "save" deer and stockpile them fail because reducing losses from one decimating factor shifts those losses to another. The bottom line is that the herd cannot exceed the carrying capacity of its habitat, at least for long.

A common tool used in deer management is to harvest animals from both sexes so that the herd can be lowered to a level slightly below the carrying capacity of its habitat. When this is achieved, deaths due to other causes are reduced. Fawn production and survival increases as the herd attempts to fill the void created by the removal of the adults through hunting. Because the deer are held to a level below the habitat capacity, there is little or no competition for food and individual animals are bigger. Of special interest to hunters, the bucks also grow bigger antlers.

With a better understanding of how deer regulate their populations around a habitat carrying capacity, we turn our attention to the factors that regulate capacity. Carrying capacity is rarely stable. Short-term changes occur as a result of weather and man's activities on the land. A wildfire, for example, might temporarily reduce the habitat on a summer range until the shrubs resprout and reproduce an increase in food above the level prior to the burn. The deer that use the area will respond to the changes by increasing in numbers.

Periodic droughts may also reduce the growth of important food plants and affect the carrying capacity of the range. Dramatic, but temporary, changes can also occur when heavy winter snows cove feeding areas for a prolonged period of time, causing deer to starve.

Winter snows, drought, and wildfire result in short-term trends in habitat capacity. More important are the long-term trends in the ability of California wildlands to support deer. Without disturbances such as lightning fires that create openings in the trees which allow young vegetation to grow, shrubs to mature and trees begin to dominate. As the canopy closes it reduces the moisture and sunlight reaching the forest floor. The habitat thus supports fewer deer.

Work throughout California and other western states confirms the shifts in habitats from mixed shrubs and trees to large areas dominated by second-growth trees and decadent brush fields. This unnatural process came about largely because of the suppression of wildfires since the middle of this century. Land managers are beginning to recognize the problems associated with the continuing suppression of natural life-giving fires on the landscape. Not only deer but many other species of plants and animals depend on periodic cleansing of the land (via fire) to create the needed mosaics of openings in the vegetative cover. Finally, we must change our attitudes about fire and learn how to reintroduce this totally natural force into the strategies we use to manage habitats.

MULE DEER

Mule Deer – Typical
Number One
Score: 195 7/8
Locality: Lassen Co.
Date: 1943
Hunter: Sulo E. Lakso

Mule Deer – Typical
Number Two
Score: 194²/₈
Locality: Siskiyou Co.
Date: 1946
Hunter: Hap Hottenstein Horn

Mule Deer – Non-Typical
Number One
Score: 319⁴/₈
Locality: Mariposa Co.
Date: 1972
Hunter: Harold R. Laird

Mule Deer – Non-Typical
Number Two
Score: 305⁶/₈
Locality: Shasta Co.
Date: 1987
Hunter: Artie McGram

Mule Deer – Non-Typical
Number Three
Score: 298 5/8
Locality: California
Date: 1940

Mule Deer – Non-Typical
Number Four
Score: 267 4/8
Locality: Mariposa County.
Date: 1948
Hunter: Ray Douglas

Mule Deer – Non-Typical
Number Five
Score: 266
Locality: Modoc County
Date: 1948
Hunter: Neil Miller

MULE DEER-TYPICAL
Odocoileus Hemionus

Score	Length of Main Beam		Inside Spread	Circumference at smallest place between burr & first point		Number of Points		Locality	Hunter	Date Killed	Rank
	Right	Left		Right	Left	Right	Left				
MULE DEER - TYPICAL ANTLERS				**Minimum Score 160**							
195 7/8	27 6/8	25 7/8	26 4/8	4 6/8	4 6/8	5	7	Lassen County, CA	Sulo E. Lakso	1943	1
194 2/8	24 2/8	24	25	5 5/8	5 5/8	5	5	Siskiyou County, CA	Hap Hottenstein	1946	2
187	26 2/8	25	21 6/8	4 6/8	4 7/8	5	7	Modoc County, CA	Don Stemler	1939	3
177 3/8	26 2/8	25 5/8	23 7/8	5 6/8	5 6/8	5	5	Modoc County, CA	Randy W. Tonkin	1993	4
164	25 4/8	24	24 4/8	4 6/8	4 5/8	5	5	Calavaras County, CA	Babe Stone	1950	5
162 7/8	21 3/8	20 4/8	18 1/8	4 3/8	4 3/8	5	4	D-7	Dave Schiavon		6
162 7/8	21 6/8	22 6/8	21 3/8	4 2/8	4 2/8	5	5	D-7	James Flamson	1982	7
160 6/8	21	21 3/8	19 6/8	4 4/8	4 4/8	5	5	Ventura County, CA	Richard Chagolla	1998	8
160 4/8	22	22 2/8	22 2/8	5 1/8	5 2/8	6	5	Calavaras County, CA	Babe Stone	1950	9
MULE DEER - NON-TYPICAL ANTLERS				**Minimum Score 190**							
319 4/8	24 2/8	24	23 5/8	7 7/8	7 1/8	27	23	Mariposa County, CA	Harold R. Laird	1972	1
305 6/8	23 7/8	24 1/8	21 3/8	6 1/8	6 4/8	17	17	Shasta County, CA	Artie McGram	1987	2
298 5/8	26 1/8	26	24 6/8	5 5/8	6	14	13	California	Unknown	1940	3
267 4/8	24	25 3/8	18 2/8	6 2/8	7 2/8	16	15	Mariposa County, CA	Ray Douglas	1948	4
266	29 7/8	30 5/8	26 7/8	4 6/8	4 6/8	10	11	Modoc County, CA	Neil Miller	1958	5
246 6/8	23 4/8	21	26 3/8	6 2/8	6 4/8	13	14	Modoc County, CA	Bill Foster	1930	6
240 4/8	26 4/8	27	21 4/8	6 2/8	5 6/8	10	9	Modoc County, CA	Niilo Niemi	1968	7
209 2/8	21 1/8	20 6/8	20	4 7/8	4 6/8	13	11	Lassen County, CA	Virgil Byers	1978	8

BLACKTAIL DEER

Columbia Blacktail Deer – Typical
Number One
Score: 175 2/8
Locality: Mendocino Co.
Date: 1981
Hunter: Clem Coughlin

Columbia Blacktail Deer – Typical
Number Two
Score: 168²/₈
Locality: Lake Co.
Date: 1953
Hunter: Bob Desheilds

Columbia Blacktail Deer – Typical
Number Three
Score: 166²/₈
Locality: Glenn Co.
Date: 1949
Hunter: Peter Gerbo

CALIFORNIA'S COASTAL BLACKTAIL

Photos taken by: Scott Wilkinson

COLUMBIA BLACKTAIL DEER
Odocoileus Hemionus Columbianus

Score	Length of Main Beam		Inside Spread	Circumference at smallest place between burr & first point		Number of Points		Locality	Hunter	Date Killed	Rank
	Right	Left		Right	Left	Right	Left				
Minimum Score 120											
175 2/8	22 5/8	22	17 1/8	4 6/8	4 6/8	6	5	Mendocino County, CA	Clem Coughlin	1981	1
168 2/8	22 4/8	21 4/8	21 4/8	5 2/8	5 1/8	5	5	Lake County, CA	Bob DeShields	1953	2
166 2/8	23 2/8	24 3/8	26 5/8	5 4/8	5 1/8	6	6	Glenn County, CA	Peter Gerbo	1949	3
164 1/8	21 2/8	20 2/8	17 5/8	4 4/8	4 4/8	5	5	Mendocino County, CA	Mervin E. Lee	1995	4
163 1/8	23 3/8	21 5/8	20 4/8	5	4 7/8	7	6	Siskiyou County, CA	Frank Barago	1945	5
162 3/8	22	22 1/8	18 1/8	4 4/8	4 4/8	5	5	Trinity County, CA	Sidney A. Nystrom	1961	6
162 2/8	24 5/8	25 1/8	19 2/8	4 2/8	4 2/8	5	5	Glenn County, CA	Roger L. Spencer	1956	7
160 4/8	23 5/8	24 3/8	21	4 7/8	4 7/8	5	6	Siskiyou County, CA	John L. Masters	1967	8
160 3/8	23 1/8	23 5/8	26 5/8	4	4	6	5	Trinity County, CA	A.H. Hilbert	1929	9
160 1/8	25 1/8	24 7/8	24 7/8	5	5 5/8	5	4	Trinity County, CA	Lorio Verzasconi	1946	10
159 7/8	22 2/8	21 7/8	16 3/8	4	4	5	5	Siskiyou County, CA	John C. Ley	1937	11
159 7/8	22 5/8	22 3/8	21 7/8	4 5/8	4 5/8	5	5	Siskiyou County, CA	Francis M. Sullivan	1951	11
159 6/8	21	21 1/8	12 3/8	5 4/8	5 5/8	5	6	Humboldt County, CA	Picked up	1968	12
159 4/8	24 4/8	23 6/8	14 7/8	4 5/8	4 4/8	6	6	Mendocino County, CA	Russ McLennan	1984	13
159 1/8	21 5/8	22 1/8	19 1/8	4 6/8	4 6/8	5	5	Trinity County, CA	A.H. Hilbert	1939	14
158 4/8	24	24 4/8	22 5/8	4 5/8	4 5/8	6	6	Trinity County, CA	David Phillips	1974	15
158	21 7/8	21 7/8	18 2/8	4 4/8	4 4/8	5	5	Trinity County, CA	Charles A. Strickland	1984	16
158	23 4/8	23	18 3/8	4 4/8	4 3/8	5	7	Siskiyou County, CA	Robert J. Ayers	1996	16
157 5/8	22 6/8	23 3/8	21 5/8	4 2/8	4 3/8	5	5	Shasta County, CA	Richard L. Sobrato	1969	17
157 2/8	21	22	21 4/8	4 4/8	4 4/8	5	5	Mendocino County, CA	Fred A. Hollenback	1956	18
157	24 7/8	26 1/8	24 1/8	5	5 1/8	5	7	Santa Clara County, CA	Brud Eade	1961	19
156 6/8	23	23 7/8	16 6/8	4 6/8	4 6/8	7	6	Trinity County, CA	Picked up	1994	20

COLUMBIA BLACKTAIL DEER
Odocoileus Hemionus Columbianus

Score	Length of Main Beam		Inside Spread	Circumference at smallest place between burr & first point		Number of Points		Locality	Hunter	Date Killed	Rank
	Right	Left		Right	Left	Right	Left				
Minimum Score 120											
155 7/8	23 1/8	23 1/8	17 3/8	4	4 2/8	5	5	Tehama County, CA	George R. Chaffin	1995	21
155 3/8	21 4/8	21	15 1/8	4 3/8	4 3/8	5	5	Tehama County, CA	Carol F. Williams	1948	22
155 2/8	21 5/8	21 6/8	23 1/8	3 3/8	3 4/8	5	5	Trinity County, CA	Fred Heider	1927	23
155 2/8	22 1/8	22 7/8	19 2/8	5 3/8	4 7/8	5	5	Mendocino County, CA	Gary Land	1972	23
155 1/8	21	21 6/8	18 5/8	4 3/8	4 3/8	4	4	Shasta County, CA	Vance Corrigan	1956	24
155 1/8	24	23	21	4 4/8	4 1/8	6	5	Tehama County, CA	Ben M. Youtsey	1995	24
154 6/8	20 4/8	20 3/8	20 4/8	4 5/8	4 5/8	4	4	Mendocino County, CA	W.A. McAllister	1968	25
154 6/8	21 1/8	21 3/8	18 1/8	4 2/8	4 2/8	6	6	Mendocino County, CA	Andy Amerson	1993	25
154 5/8	24	22 7/8	23 3/8	4 3/8	4 4/8	5	5	Humboldt County, CA	Phillip Brown	1962	26
154 5/8	24 7/8	24 3/8	21	4 7/8	4 6/8	6	7	Siskiyou County, CA	Darrell R. Jones	1984	26
154 1/8	21 6/8	22 2/8	18 6/8	4 6/8	4 7/8	6	7	Glenn County, CA	Mitchell A. Thorson	1969	27
154	26 4/8	25 7/8	28 6/8	4 4/8	4 6/8	6	6	Trinity County, CA	A.H. Hilbert	1930	28
154	22	23 7/8	22 2/8	4 3/8	4 4/8	5	4	Mendocino County, CA	William E. Soekland	1994	28
153 3/8	21 2/8	21 5/8	17 4/8	5	5	6	5	Tehama County, CA	James L. Carr	1979	29
153 1/8	20 2/8	20	17 1/8	4 6/8	4 6/8	5	5	Humboldt County, CA	Paul M. Mustain	1975	30
153	22 6/8	23 6/8	14 6/8	4 3/8	4 5/8	6	6	Siskiyou County, CA	John Carmichael	1969	31
152 6/8	21 6/8	21 7/8	21 1/8	4 6/8	4 3/8	8	7	Tehama County, CA	Randy E. Reno	1995	32
152 5/8	21 7/8	20 4/8	20 5/8	4 4/8	4 5/8	5	5	W. Stanislaus County, CA	Scott A. Wilkinson	1998	33
152 5/8	23 6/8	22 7/8	18 5/8	5	5 2/8	5	4	Trinity County, CA	Allen Brownfield	1979	33
152 5/8	22 1/8	22	19 5/8	4	4 3/8	5	5	Mendocino County, CA	Harold D. Schneider	1979	33
152 5/8	23 6/8	22 7/8	18 5/8	5	5 2/8	5	4	Trinity County, CA	Larry Brown	1979	33
152 4/8	23	23	20	4	4	6	7	Tehama County, CA	Don Strickler	1979	34
152 4/8	22	21 2/8	18 4/8	5 1/8	5	6	6	Mendocino County, CA	Richard C. Martin	1990	34

Score								Location	Name	Year	Rank
152 1/8	22 4/8	21 4/8	17 7/8	4 2/8	4 1/8	5	5	Trinity County, CA	Robert V. Strickland	1966	35
152	23 3/8	22 7/8	21 6/8	4 4/8	4 4/8	5	5	Yolo County, CA	Herman Darneille	1943	36
151 7/8	21 6/8	22	20 1/8	5	5	6	5	Tehama County, CA	Gerald R. Cardoza, Jr.	1994	37
151 6/8	24 6/8	25	23 6/8	4 1/8	4 2/8	3	4	Stanislaus County, CA	Picked up	1998	38
151 5/8	20 3/8	20 1/8	22 4/8	4 5/8	4 4/8	5	5	Mendocino County, CA	Bill L. Conn	1969	39
151 5/8	22 1/8	21 7/8	22 5/8	4 6/8	4 6/8	5	5	Siskiyou County, CA	Jim A. Turnbow	1973	39
151 5/8	21	21 3/8	15 5/8	4 1/8	4	5	5	Trinity County, CA	Dean Giordanella	1994	39
151	20 1/8	21	19 2/8	4 2/8	4 1/8	5	5	Humboldt County, CA	Elgin T. Gates	1952	40
150 6/8	22	21 4/8	17	4 2/8	4 2/8	5	5	Siskiyou County, CA	Raymond Whittaker	1978	41
150 6/8	21 6/8	22 2/8	18 3/8	4 7/8	4 6/8	6	5	Santa Clara County, CA	Robert L. Fellom	1997	41
150 4/8	24 1/8	24 2/8	19 5/8	5 1/8	5	6	6	Trinity County, CA	E.L. Brightenstine	1978	42
150 1/8	22 4/8	22	16 1/8	4 1/8	4 1/8	5	5	Napa County, CA	Robert G. Wiley	1965	43
150 1/8	21	21	20 1/8	3 7/8	3 7/8	5	5	Trinity County, CA	Thomas L. Hough	1969	43
150	24	25 5/8	24	4 5/8	4 4/8	4	4	Napa County, CA	W.C. Lambert	1957	44
150	20 7/8	20 2/8	20	5 3/8	5 3/8	4	4	Lake County, CA	Bruce Strickler	1970	44
150	20 4/8	21 7/8	16 6/8	4 2/8	4 2/8	5	5	Tehama County, CA	Marion F. Foster	1971	44
150	21 5/8	21 4/8	21 2/8	4 2/8	4 2/8	5	5	Trinity County, CA	Richard E. Keller	1995	44
149 7/8	23 2/8	22 5/8	17 3/8	4 1/8	4 2/8	6	5	Siskiyou County, CA	John R. Adams	1985	45
149 7/8	21 2/8	20 4/8	16 1/8	4 1/8	4 2/8	5	5	Trinity County, CA	Steven E. Delaney	1992	45
149 6/8	22 7/8	22	18 7/8	5	5	6	6	Siskiyou County, CA	Emit C. Jones	1961	46
149 5/8	20	21 3/8	17 7/8	4 4/8	4 4/8	5	5	Humboldt County, CA	Robert C. Stephens	1961	47
149 4/8	22 5/8	21	20 6/8	5 2/8	5 1/8	5	5	Glenn County, CA	George Stewart, Jr	1957	48
149 4/8	21 1/8	21 4/8	23	5	5 1/8	5	5	Mendocino County, CA	C.W. Bill King	1993	48
149 3/8	22 3/8	21 2/8	20 3/8	5 4/8	5 2/8	5	5	Trinity County, CA	Lyle L. Johnson	1979	49
149 3/8	23 7/8	26 5/8	20 5/8	4 4/8	4 5/8	5	5	Tehama County, CA	Bill F. Stevenson	1989	49
149 2/8	24 3/8	24 3/8	17 6/8	5 4/8	5 4/8	8	8	Trinity County, CA	Lauren A. Johnson	1964	50
148 7/8	22 1/8	21 3/8	18	4 7/8	4 7/8	6	5	Humboldt County, CA	F. Joe Parker	1946	51
148 6/8	22 5/8	22 6/8	15 6/8	4 6/8	4 6/8	5	5	Trinity County, CA	Donald A. Dunn	1993	52
148 4/8	23 2/8	22 7/8	20 6/8	4 5/8	4 3/8	5	5	Mendocino County, CA	N.D. Windbigler	1969	53
148 2/8	24	24 4/8	23 4/8	5 6/8	6 2/8	6	6	Shasta County, CA	Jerry W. Sander	1977	54

COLUMBIA BLACKTAIL DEER
Odocoileus Hemionus Columbianus

Score	Length of Main Beam		Inside Spread	Circumference at smallest place between burr & first point		Number of Points		Locality	Hunter	Date Killed	Rank
	Right	Left		Right	Left	Right	Left				
Minimum Score 120											
155 7/8	23 1/8	23 1/8	17 3/8	4	4 2/8	5	5	Tehama County, CA	George R. Chaffin	1995	21
148 1/8	21 6/8	22 1/8	18 6/8	5	5 1/8	8	7	Trinity County, CA	Dean Tackette	1981	55
147 7/8	22	22 3/8	18 5/8	4 1/8	4 2/8	5	5	Glenn County, CA	Emmet T. Frye	1937	56
147 7/8	20 6/8	20 7/8	21 6/8	5	4 7/8	5	5	Trinity County, CA	Chauncy Willburn	1955	56
147 7/8	22 1/8	22 2/8	18 5/8	4 2/8	4 3/8	6	6	Humboldt County, CA	Melvin H. Kadle	1979	56
147 7/8	19 7/8	21 7/8	22 1/8	4 6/8	4 7/8	6	5	Siskiyou County, CA	James C. Elliott	1974	56
147 5/8	23	23 6/8	19 5/8	4 4/8	4 3/8	5	4	Santa Clara County, CA	Maitland Armstrong	1944	57
147 5/8	22 3/8	22 7/8	22 3/8	4 5/8	4 5/8	4	4	Mendocino County, CA	Richard Sterling	1986	57
147 4/8	21 4/8	22 1/8	16 4/8	4	4	5	5	Mendocino County, CA	Picked up	1995	58
147 1/8	21 2/8	21	16 7/8	4 3/8	4 3/8	5	6	Trinity County, CA	Craig L. Brown	1980	59
147 1/8	22 4/8	23 3/8	21 7/8	4 2/8	4 5/8	6	5	Trinity County, CA	Barry D. Keyes	1992	59
147	18	18 2/8	17	4 3/8	4 2/8	5	5	Siskiyou County, CA	Ray Whittaker	1966	60
147	22 2/8	22 3/8	19 6/8	4 3/8	4 3/8	5	5	Mendocino County, CA	David W. Wilson	1993	60
146 6/8	20	20 4/8	18 4/8	4 3/8	4 3/8	5	5	Siskiyou County, CA	Richard Silva	1958	61
146 4/8	21 2/8	21 2/8	17 2/8	4 6/8	4 7/8	5	5	Glenn County, CA	Lawrence E. Germeshausen	1983	62
146 3/8	23 4/8	23 6/8	24 6/8	4 5/8	4 5/8	5	5	Trinity County, CA	Carroll E. Dow	1962	63
146 3/8	21 5/8	22	17 5/8	3 5/8	3 6/8	5	5	Trinity County, CA	David J. Deininger	1992	63
146 2/8	21 6/8	22 3/8	13 6/8	5 6/8	5 6/8	5	5	Shasta County, CA	William H. Taylor	1971	64
146 2/8	21 7/8	21 6/8	16 2/8	3 7/8	3 7/8	5	5	Humboldt County, CA	Charles R. Jurin	1988	64
146 1/8	23 1/8	23 5/8	19 1/8	4 5/8	4	4	4	Trinity County, CA	Kenneth M. Brown	1972	65
146 1/8	22 2/8	23 4/8	19 1/8	3 7/8	4 2/8	4	5	Mendocino County, CA	Brad B. Pitt	1994	65
146	22 6/8	22 2/8	19 2/8	4 4/8	4 5/8	5	5	Mendocino County, CA	Brian E. Hornberger	1991	66
146	20 5/8	21 5/8	21 4/8	4 3/8	4 2/8	5	5	Mendocino County, CA	Renaldo J. Marin	1993	66

146	22	21	22	4 2/8	4 2/8	5	5	Mendocino County, CA	Cliff E. Jacobson	1996	66
145 7/8	23 4/8	23 3/8	22	5 3/8	5 4/8	6	8	Lake County, CA	Floyd Goodrich	1926	67
145 7/8	22	23 5/8	16 3/8	4 5/8	4 7/8	5	5	Napa County, CA	C.H. N.Dailey	1948	67
145 7/8	22 6/8	22 6/8	21 7/8	4 3/8	4 5/8	5	5	Shasta County, CA	Gary J. Miller	1968	67
145 5/8	22 4/8	23	18 7/8	4 1/8	4 1/8	6	5	Humboldt County, CA	Joe Dickerson	1962	68
145 5/8	21 2/8	21 1/8	19 5/8	3 7/8	4	5	5	Siskiyou County, CA	Wallace D. Barlow	1985	68
145 4/8	21 3/8	21 1/8	21 3/8	4 5/8	4 7/8	5	6	Mendocino County, CA	Kenneth A. Bovers	1993	69
145 3/8	22 3/8	21	23 4/8	4 5/8	4 6/8	5	5	Mendocino County, CA	Paul M. Holleman II	1976	70
145 3/8	23 3/8	22	22 6/8	4 1/8	4	6	5	Trinity County, CA	Donald A. Dunn	1992	70
145 3/8	22 4/8	22 5/8	21	5 3/8	5 1/8	7	9	Tehama County, CA	Clint Heiber	1979	71
145 2/8	24 4/8	24 4/8	21 7/8	4 2/8	4 3/8	5	4	Trinity County, CA	Chris Smith	1996	71
145 2/8	23 5/8	23 4/8	23 3/8	5 1/8	5 2/8	5	5	Tehama County, CA	Lamar G. Hanson	1972	72
145 1/8	21 4/8	20 7/8	19 4/8	4 3/8	4 3/8	5	6	Trinity County, CA	Gene Shannon	1990	72
145 1/8	19 6/8	21 7/8	17 1/8	4 7/8	5 1/8	6	6	Humboldt County, CA	Marvin D. Stapp	1965	73
145	22 2/8	21 4/8	21 2/8	5 1/8	5 1/8	7	5	Mendocino County, CA	Ralph I. Sibley	1986	73
145	22 2/8	22 4/8	22 4/8	4 4/8	4 6/8	5	5	Mendocino County, CA	Richard Vannelli	1970	74
144 6/8	21	20	18	4 3/8	4 2/8	5	5	Santa Clara County, CA	Dean P. Filice	1996	74
144 6/8	21 1/8	20 6/8	14	4 2/8	4 2/8	5	5	Siskiyou County, CA	William G. Jarrell	1997	74
144 6/8	21 4/8	21 3/8	19 4/8	4 3/8	4 3/8	5	5	Shasta County, CA	Ernie Young	1953	75
144 4/8	20 4/8	20 7/8	14 7/8	4 4/8	4 5/8	5	5	Humboldt County, CA	Richard G. Van Vorst	1990	76
144 3/8	20 1/8	22	19 1/8	4 4/8	4 4/8	5	5	Alameda County, CA	Anthony S. Webb	1990	76
144 3/8	21	20 7/8	16 5/8	4 7/8	4 5/8	5	5	Humboldt County, CA	Gerald Wescott	1980	76
144 3/8	22 1/8	23 3/8	21 3/8	5	5 2/8	5	5	Santa Clara County, CA	Maitland Armstrong	1946	76
144 2/8	21	22 4/8	20 4/8	4 4/8	4 4/8	5	4	Mendocino County, CA	Frank Kester	1981	77
143 7/8	20 5/8	19 5/8	20 3/8	5	5 1/8	5	5	Humboldt County, CA	Lois C. Miller	1986	78
143 6/8	20 6/8	20 3/8	15 4/8	5 2/8	4 7/8	5	5	Humboldt County, CA	Hartwell A. Burnett	1988	79
143 6/8	20 5/8	20 2/8	19 7/8	5 2/8	5 2/8	6	5	Tehama County, CA	Clint Heiber	1978	79
143 6/8	19 5/8	19 4/8	15 2/8	4 7/8	4 6/8	5	6	Mendocino County, CA	Mark Ciancio	1986	79
143 5/8	20 4/8	20 4/8	18 5/8	4 4/8	4 4/8	4	4	Siskiyou County, CA	Emit C. Jones	1960	80
143 5/8	20 5/8	19 3/8	18 5/8	4 1/8	4 2/8	5	5	Trinity County, CA	Kenneth L. Cogle, Jr.	1985	80

COLUMBIA BLACKTAIL DEER
Odocoileus Hemionus Columbianus

Score	Length of Main Beam Right	Left	Inside Spread	Circumference at smallest place between burr & first point Right	Left	Number of Points Right	Left	Locality	Hunter	Date Killed	Rank
Minimum Score 120											
143 4/8	22 6/8	22 4/8	20	4 2/8	4 3/8	5	5	Mendocino County, CA	Arnold E. Dado	1993	81
143 4/8	21	20 4/8	17	4 6/8	4 6/8	5	5	Trinity County, CA	Barry Griffin	1983	81
143 3/8	19 2/8	18 7/8	18 3/8	3 4/8	3 4/8	5	5	Mendocino County, CA	Larry G. Miller	1978	82
143 2/8	20	20 2/8	15 6/8	4 2/8	4	5	5	Shasta County, CA	Ben Brackett	1993	83
143 2/8	20 3/8	20 4/8	15	4 6/8	4 7/8	8	7	Shasta County, CA	Brad E. Wittner	1989	83
143 2/8	26	26	25	4 6/8	4 6/8	5	6	Mendocino County, CA	George W. Rogers	1977	83
143 2/8	19 5/8	19 4/8	17 2/8	4	4	5	5	Humboldt County, CA	Jack Stedman	1965	83
143 2/8	22 3/8	22 6/8	21 4/8	4 2/8	4 2/8	5	5	Lake County, CA	Mario Sereni, Jr	1965	83
143 1/8	21 6/8	22 2/8	17 1/8	4 1/8	4 1/8	5	5	Humboldt County, CA	Eddie L. Mendes	1992	84
143 1/8	22	22 1/8	18 1/8	4 1/8	4	5	5	Humboldt County, CA	Mitchell A. Thorson	1965	84
142 7/8	23 1/8	22 4/8	17 3/8	4	4 2/8	5	5	Tehama County, CA	Randy Croote	1993	85
142 6/8	20 1/8	20 2/8	20 5/8	5 4/8	5 6/8	5	5	Mendocino County, CA	Steen C. Henriksen	1996	86
142 5/8	20 2/8	20	16 5/8	4 1/8	4	5	5	Santa Clara County, CA	Picked up	PR 196687	87
142 5/8	22 5/8	22 6/8	19 7/8	4 2/8	4 2/8	5	5	Santa Clara County, CA	Picked up	PR 196687	87
142 5/8	21 4/8	20 3/8	19 7/8	4 4/8	4 3/8	4	4	Trinity County, CA	Larry Brown	1979	87
142 5/8	23 1/8	22 1/8	20 1/8	4 6/8	4 7/8	7	6	Tehama County, CA	Kenneth R. Hall	1979	87
142 5/8	22	23	20 5/8	4	3	5	5	Mendocino County, CA	Warren F. Coffman	1989	87
142 5/8	20	20 6/8	17 7/8	4 2/8	4 1/8	5	5	Trinity County, CA	Robert T. Edwards	1991	87
142 4/8	22 2/8	22 6/8	13 3/8	4 6/8	4 6/8	4	5	Trinity County, CA	Jace Comfort	1965	88
142 4/8	21 1/8	20 4/8	15 4/8	4 6/8	4 6/8	5	5	Mendocino County, CA	Jerry C. Russell	1993	88
142 3/8	20 6/8	20 7/8	17 3/8	4 3/8	4 5/8	5	5	Laytonville, CA	Bryon J. Rowland, Jr.	1964	89
142 3/8	23	22	19 3/8	4	4	5	5	Humboldt County, CA	Darol L. Damm	1976	89
142 3/8	20 6/8	20 5/8	19 1/8	4 6/8	4 5/8	5	5	Humboldt County, CA	James L. Sloan	1992	89

Score								Name	Location	Year	Rank
142 2/8	23 4/8	23 2/8	17	4 2/8	4 1/8	6	5	James A. Shelton	Mendocino County, CA	1944	90
142 2/8	20 7/8	20 6/8	19 6/8	4	4 1/8	6	6	Donald A. Dunn	Trinity County, CA	1981	90
142 1/8	22	22	20 3/8	4 3/8	4 1/8	4	4	John T. Scheffler	Siskiyou County, CA	1992	91
142 1/8	20 4/8	20 2/8	15 3/8	4 2/8	4	6	8	Michael R. Weber	Tehama County, CA	1996	91
142 1/8	21 3/8	22 3/8	19 7/8	5 1/8	5 1/8	5	4	Richard R. Lowell	Shasta County, CA	1953	91
141 7/8	21 4/8	21 2/8	17 7/8	4 7/8	5	5	5	Pedro H. Henrich	Trinity County, CA	1977	92
141 7/8	21 6/8	21 4/8	17 6/8	3 7/8	4	6	5	Melvin M. Clair	Trinity County, CA	1992	92
141 7/8	19 7/8	19 6/8	20 3/8	4	4 2/8	5	5	A.H. Bilbert	Trinity County, CA	PR 195593	92
141 5/8	21 1/8	21 6/8	18 5/8	3 6/8	3 6/8	5	5	Lanny G. King	Mendocino County, CA	1992	93
141 4/8	21 2/8	21 1/8	16 2/8	4 2/8	4 2/8	5	5	Greg Rocha	Mendocino County, CA	1985	94
141 4/8	20 7/8	20 4/8	20	4 4/8	4 4/8	5	5	Les Johnson	Del Norte County, CA	1986	94
141 3/8	22 1/8	21 5/8	18 7/8	4 7/8	4 5/8	5	4	Larry Brown	Trinity County, CA	1980	95
141 3/8	21 2/8	21 7/8	16 7/8	4 3/8	4 1/8	5	5	Gene V. Bradley	Mendocino County, CA	1988	95
141 2/8	21 4/8	20 4/8	18	4 2/8	4 4/8	5	5	Barry D. Keyes	Trinity County, CA	1989	96
141 2/8	21 5/8	21 4/8	16	3 6/8	4	5	5	Donald A. Dunn	Trinity County, CA	1996	96
141		21 1/8	17	3 7/8	4 1/8	5	5	Allen Pierce, Jr.	Humboldt County, CA	1959	97
141	21	20 2/8	19 4/8	4 4/8	4	5	4	Richard Vannelli	Mendocino County, CA	1970	97
141	23	24 4/8	22	5 4/8	5 4/8	7	6	Gerald W. Whitmire	Mendocino County, CA	1976	97
141	22 4/8	21 3/8	20	4 3/8	3 6/8	5	4	Richard L. Valladao	Mendocino County, CA	1993	97
141	18 4/8	18 6/8	13	4 4/8	4 3/8	5	5	Charles Nesler	Santa Clara County, CA	1957	97
140 7/8	21 1/8	20 1/8	21 1/8	4 3/8	4 4/8	5	5	Dave Swenson	Shasta County, CA	1968	98
140 7/8	23 3/8	22	16 5/8	3 7/8	4	5	5	Doughlas W. Lim	Mendocino County, CA	1981	98
140 6/8	21	22 2/8	20 6/8	4	5 1/8	5	5	Bill L. Conn	Mendocino County, CA	1968	99
140 6/8	23 4/8	23	18 6/8	4 6/8	5 4/8	5	4	Robert Lynch	Mendocino County, CA	1971	99
140 6/8	23	22 4/8	20	5 4/8	5	5	5	Jerry D. Smith	Mendocino County, CA	1978	99
140 6/8	21 3/8	22 1/8	16 1/8	4 4/8	4 5/8	6	7	H. James Tonkin, Jr.	Trinity County, CA	1995	99
140 5/8	23	21 7/8	18 3/8	4 6/8	4 4/8	5	5	Luther Clements	Shasta County, CA	1944	100
140 4/8	19 4/8	20	17 2/8	4 4/8	4 1/8	5	5	Loran G. August	Trinity County, CA	1980	101
140 4/8	21 1/8	21 3/8	14 2/8	4 1/8	4 2/8	5	5	Jay M. Gates III	Mendocino County, CA	1986	101
140 4/8	20 5/8	22	15	4 1/8	4 2/8	5	5	Jerry R. Cardoza	Trinity County, CA	1996	101

COLUMBIA BLACKTAIL DEER
Odocoileus Hemionus Columbianus

Score	Length of Main Beam Right	Left	Inside Spread	Circumference at smallest place between burr & first point Right	Left	Number of Points Right	Left	Locality	Hunter	Date Killed	Rank
Minimum Score 120											
140 3/8	20 1/8	20 5/8	16 5/8	3 7/8	4 3/8	4	5	Humboldt County, CA	George S. Johnson	1934	102
140 3/8	22	21	17 7/8	4	4	5	5	Siskiyou County, CA	Rodney Irwin	1966	102
140 2/8	21	20 7/8	19 6/8	5	4 6/8	5	5	Mendocino County, CA	Harry S. Richardson	1952	103
140 2/8	21 4/8	21 4/8	19 6/8	3 7/8	3 7/8	5	5	Mendocino County, CA	Earl E. Hamlow, Jr.	1977	103
140 2/8	22	21 4/8	23 4/8	4 3/8	4 3/8	4	5	Trinity County, CA	Charles E. Davy	1983	103
140 1/8	21 2/8	21 5/8	15 6/8	4 2/8	4 2/8	5	7	Mendocino County, CA	Clarence W. Nelson	1948	104
140 1/8	20 4/8	19 4/8	16 3/8	4 3/8	4 2/8	4	4	Santa Clara County, CA	Dick Sullivan	1977	104
140 1/8	21 1/8	20 2/8	16 3/8	3 7/8	4	4	4	Siskiyou County, CA	Richford M. Fisher	1986	104
140 1/8	21 6/8	21	17 1/8	4	4 4/8	5	6	Trinity County, CA	Wayne Jorensen	1986	104
140 1/8	18 4/8	18 1/8	17 3/8	4 2/8	4 3/8	5	5	Santa Clara County, CA	Darin S. Filice	1995	104
140	20 2/8	20 2/8	16	4 7/8	4 6/8	7	5	Mendocino County, CA	Roy Bergstrom	1966	105
140	22 4/8	22 2/8	18	5 5/8	5 2/8	5	5	Mendocino County, CA	Nick Deffterios	1970	105
140	22	21 3/8	17 6/8	4 1/8	4 1/8	5	5	Humboldt County, CA	Carl A. Anderson	1980	105
140	21 5/8	22 1/8	19	3 7/8	4 2/8	4	5	Trinity County, CA	William J. Olson	1981	105
140	20 4/8	21 4/8	17 2/8	4	3 6/8	7	5	Siskiyou County, CA	Doug Weinrich	1993	105
139 7/8	19	18 6/8	15 5/8	4	4	4	5	Siskiyou County, CA	Roy Eastlick	1954	106
139 7/8	22 1/8	20 7/8	21 3/8	5 1/8	5	4	5	Trinity County, CA	Craig L. Brown	1981	106
139 7/8	12 4/8	22	18 1/8	4 1/8	4 1/8	5	5	Mendocino County, CA	David A. Chandler	1997	106
139 7/8	20 5/8	20 2/8	17 5/8	6	5 5/8	6	8	Humboldt County, CA	Jace Comfort	1997	106
139 6/8	21 5/8	22 4/8	16	4 1/8	4	5	5	Shasta County, CA	Warren Hunter	1964	107
139 6/8	22 2/8	22 5/8	21 4/8	3 3/8	3 5/8	5	5	Trinity County, CA	Andrew C. Hiebert	1993	107
139 4/8	22	22 3/8	20	4 1/8	4 2/8	5	5	Humboldt County, CA	Robert B. Feamster	1996	108
139 4/8	20 2/8	22	15 6/8	4 3/8	4 2/8	5	5	Mendocino County, CA	Jack J. Tuso	1996	108

139 3/8	19 4/8	19 5/8	20 6/8	4 2/8	6	5	Mendocino County, CA	Walter R. Schubert	1952	109
139 3/8	24 5/8	23 3/8	21 5/8	4 7/8	5	5	Trinity County, CA	Andy Burgess	1964	109
139 3/8	21 4/8	21 5/8	22 5/8	4 3/8	5	5	Siskiyou County, CA	Loren L. Lutz	1964	109
139 3/8	21	21	19 1/8	4 5/8	5	5	Mendocino County, CA	Richard L. Moore	1992	109
139 2/8	18 7/8	19 4/8	14 6/8	3 6/8	4	4	Trinity County, CA	Donald A. Dunn	1960	110
139 2/8	21 3/8	21 4/8	20 1/8	4 1/8	5	4	Humboldt County, CA	Jeff Bryant	1964	110
139 2/8	22 5/8	21 1/8	18 6/8	3 5/8	4	6	Trinity County, CA	Gary L. Mayberry	1968	110
139 2/8	21	21	16 7/8	3 7/8	5	6	Trinity County, CA	Terry H. Walker	1986	110
139 2/8	20 5/8	20 4/8	20	4 1/8	4	4	Humboldt County, CA	Daniel D. Zent	1991	110
139 2/8	22	21 1/8	18 6/8	4 4/8	6	6	Siskiyou County, CA	Thomas K. Higgs	1993	110
139 1/8	22	21 2/8	18 5/8	4 2/8	5	5	Humboldt County, CA	George E. Watson	1933	111
139 1/8	22 1/8	22	17 5/8	4	4	5	Mendocino County, CA	John Winn, Jr.	1972	111
139 1/8	23 2/8	23 3/8	20 3/8	5 3/8	5	5	Santa Clara County, CA	Jack G. James	1945	111
139	22	21 6/8	17 2/8	4	4	4	Trinity County, CA	Roger J. Scala	1990	112
138 7/8	21	22 2/8	20 5/8	4 2/8	4	4	Siskiyou County, CA	Darrell Nowdesha	1961	113
138 7/8	19 1/8	20 5/8	15 3/8	4 5/8	4	5	Trinity County, CA	William O. Louderback	1963	113
138 7/8	21 3/8	21 7/8	19 5/8	5	6	5	Mendocino County, CA	Donald W. Biggs	1992	113
138 6/8	21 3/8	20 4/8	16	4 1/8	4	5	Humboldt County, CA	Larry Bowermaster	1964	114
138 6/8	22 2/8	21 1/8	22 2/8	4	5	5	Mendocino County, CA	Gordon O. Hanson	1988	114
138 6/8	18 4/8	18	16 2/8	3 7/8	5	5	Mendocino County, CA	Richard L. Moore	1988	114
138 6/8	22 3/8	25 2/8	20 6/8	3 6/8	4	4	Mendocino County, CA	Thomas R. Erasmy	1993	114
138 4/8	22 4/8	22 7/8	18 6/8	4	5	4	Mendocino County, CA	Jess Jones	1950	115
138 4/8	21 1/8	20	18 2/8	4 3/8	5	5	Siskiyou County, CA	Bob Courts	1965	115
138 4/8	19 4/8	19 4/8	17 2/8	4	5	6	Siskiyou County, CA	John Carmichael	1969	115
138 4/8	20 5/8	20 7/8	18	4 5/8	5	5	Mendocino County, CA	John D. Tuso	1997	115
138 3/8	22 4/8	22 2/8	18	4 4/8	5	5	Humboldt County, CA	Gary Hughes	1968	116
138 3/8	20 4/8	20 1/8	18 5/8	4 1/8	4	5	Trinity County, CA	Stanley A. Apuli	1991	116
138 2/8	21 4/8	22	18 2/8	4 3/8	5	5	Trinity County, CA	E.G. Palmrose	1940	117
138 2/8	21 3/8	21 3/8	15 6/8	5 3/8	5	5	Tehama County, CA	Robert L. Armanasco	1968	117
138 2/8	21 5/8	22	17 6/8	3 6/8	5	5	Trinity County, CA	Thomas R. Pettigrew, Jr.	1972	117

COLUMBIA BLACKTAIL DEER

Odocoileus Hemionus Columbianus

Score	Length of Main Beam		Inside Spread	Circumference at smallest place between burr & first point		Number of Points		Locality	Hunter	Date Killed	Rank
	Right	Left		Right	Left	Right	Left				
Minimum Score 120											
138 2/8	18	18	14 4/8	4 4/8	4 1/8	5	5	Mendocino County, CA	Kenzia L. Brake	1985	117
138 2/8	19 5/8	20 4/8	16 2/8	4 3/8	4 3/8	5	5	Trinity County, CA	Monte D. Matheson	1990	117
138	22 3/8	21 7/8	21 1/8	4 7/8	5	5	6	Mendocino County, CA	Brain K. Isaac	1985	118
137 7/8	20 4/8	19 4/8	18 6/8	4	4 2/8	6	5	Shasta County, CA	Paul G. Carter	1964	119
137 7/8	18 4/8	17 5/8	17 3/8	4	4	5	5	Trinity County, CA	Picked up	1965	119
137 7/8	18	18 5/8	18 5/8	5	4 5/8	4	4	Santa Clara County, CA	Farbert L. Johnston	1967	119
137 7/8	21	21	16	5	4 7/8	5	6	Trinity County, CA	Daniel M. Phillips	1993	119
137 7/8	20 1/8	20 3/8	16 1/8	4	4	5	5	Humboldt County, CA	Michael M. Golightly	1991	119
137 6/8	19 1/8	19 6/8	16 6/8	4	4	4	4	Siskiyou County, CA	Robert L. Miller	1985	120
137 6/8	20 2/8	20 7/8	19 6/8	3 6/8	3 7/8	4	5	Trinity County, CA	Kevin Clair	1986	120
137 6/8	20 5/8	20 2/8	18 6/8	3 5/8	3 5/8	5	5	Trinity County, CA	Gary A. Bradford	1996	120
137 5/8	20 4/8	20 3/8	19 5/8	4 4/8	4 5/8	5	5	Mendocino County, CA	P.R. Borton	1965	121
137 5/8	19 7/8	19 5/8	17 5/8	4 4/8	4 6/8	7	5	Napa County, CA	Bruce D. Ringsmith	1967	121
137 5/8	20 3/8	21 1/8	20 7/8	4 1/8	4	4	4	Trinity County, CA	Kenzia L. Drake	1994	121
137 4/8	19 3/8	19	17	4 1/8	4 1/8	5	5	Trinity County, CA	Philip Grunert	1967	122
137 4/8	21 1/8	21 1/8	19	4 1/8	4 3/8	5	5	Trinity County, CA	Picked up	1982	122
137 4/8	20 2/8	20 3/8	20 2/8	4 4/8	4 4/8	4	5	Santa Clara County, CA	Rayle Deit	1997	122
137 3/8	20 4/8	21 2/8	19 1/8	4 6/8	4 6/8	5	5	Trinity County, CA	Donald A. Dunn	1977	123
137 3/8	20 4/8	21 7/8	18 7/8	4 6/8	4 5/8	5	5	Mendocino County, CA	Carlton C. White	1983	123
137 3/8	20 6/8	21 2/8	17 6/8	4 1/8	4 1/8	6	5	Trinity County, CA	Robert E. Fulmer	1993	123
137 2/8	21 6/8	22 3/8	16 6/8	4 3/8	4 3/8	5	5	Lake County, CA	Kevin R. Smith	1997	124
137 1/8	20	20 5/8	23 2/8	4 3/8	4 3/8	5	6	Shasta County, CA	Jack Floyd	1957	125
137 1/8	23	22 4/8	22 7/8	5	4 6/8	5	4	Tehama County, CA	Clint Heiber	1977	125

Rank	Year	Hunter	Location	R	L						Score
126	1962	Shirley Eastlick	Siskiyou County, CA	5	5	3 6/8	3 7/8	21 6/8	21	20 4/8	137
126	1991	Shelby Bagley	Mendocino County, CA	4	4	4 7/8	4 7/8	19 2/8	21 3/8	22	137
127	1976	Danny Payne	Santa Clara County, CA	5	5	4 1/8	4 2/8	13 7/8	22 1/8	19 7/8	136 6/8
127	1957	Vance Corrigan	Shasta County, CA	4	4	4 6/8	4 7/8	18 2/8	23	21 6/8	136 6/8
128	1960	Charles Tollini	Ukiah, CA	5	5	4 4/8	4 4/8	18	20 1/8	20 3/8	136 4/8
128	1993	Jeff P. Leyden	Mendocino County, CA	4	5	4 7/8	5	18 4/8	22	22	136 4/8
128	1976	Danny Payne	Santa Clara County, CA	5	5	4 1/8	4 2/8	13 7/8	22 1/8	19 7/8	136 4/8
129	1967	David G. Cox	Cavelo, CA	4	4	4 1/8	3 6/8	20 2/8	20 4/8	20 6/8	136 2/8
129	1977	Wayne G. Rose	Siskiyou County, CA	5	5	4 7/8	5	21 4/8	22	21 6/8	136 2/8
129	1997	Denyse C. Linde	Mendocino County, CA	5	5	4 4/8	4 3/8	19 2/8	20 1/8	19 6/8	136 2/8
129	1941	Glenn Brem	Santa Clara County, CA	4	5	4 4/8	4 4/8	21 5/8	21 3/8	21 4/8	136 2/8
130	1956	Mrs. Maitland Armstrong	Santa Clara County, CA	6	6	5 1/8	5 1/8	19	23	21 6/8	136
130	1966	Edward Q. Garayalde	Mendocino County, CA	5	5	4 3/8	4 4/8	17	21	21 4/8	136
130	1968	Robert L. Armanasco	Tehama County, CA	4	5	4 7/8	4 6/8	19 2/8	21	21 4/8	136
130	1973	Dan Caughey, Sr.	San Mateo County, CA	3	3	4 6/8	4 7/8	21 6/8	23	23 1/8	136
130	1973	Richard G. Shelton	Trinity County, CA	6	6	4 1/8	4 1/8	19	19 2/8	20 4/8	136
130	1987	John P. Morton	Trinity County, CA	6	5	4	4	19 2/8	19 6/8	20 4/8	136
130	1996	George A. Deffterios	Mendocino County, CA	5	5	4 2/8	4 1/8	19 2/8	19 6/8	18 7/8	136
131	1982	John A. Crockett	Tehama County, CA	4	4	4 2/8	4 2/8	16 1/8	19 3/8	19 2/8	135 7/8
132	1965	Roy J. Renner	Trinity County, CA	4	5	3 3/8	3 4/8	19 4/8	20 1/8	20 2/8	135 6/8
132	1992	Phyllis W. Stevenson	Mendocino County, CA	5	5	4 1/8	4 2/8	16	205	20 4/8	135 6/8
133	1990	Michael M. Golightly	Humboldt County, CA	5	5	4 1/8	4 1/8	15 1/8	21 2/8	20 2/8	135 5/8
133	1990	Ray D. MacDonald, Jr.	Mendocino County, CA	4	4	4 4/8	4 7/8	20 4/8	23 6/8	23 7/8	135 5/8
134	1988	Robert T. Hammaker	Trinity County, CA	5	5	4 3/8	4 3/8	17 4/8	20 6/8	20 1/8	135 4/8
134	1996	Richy Stoddard	Mendocino County, CA	4	5	4 3/8	4 2/8	16	18 3/8	18 3/8	135 4/8
135	1996	Steve Smith	Trinity County, CA	5	5	5 1/8	4 6/8	16	20 4/8	20 4/8	135 3/8
136	1996	Andy Burgess	Trinity County, CA	5	5	3 3/8	3 4/8	15	20	19 6/8	135 2/8
136	1959	Christopher A. Umbertus	Humboldt County, CA	4	4	3 4/8	3 4/8	13 2/8	19 4/8	19 1/8	135 2/8
136	1981	Richard J. Banko, Jr.	Humboldt County, CA	4	5	4 2/8	4 2/8	18 6/8	21 1/8	21	135 2/8
137	1997	Michael L. Rudick	Trinity County, CA	5	5	4 6/8	4 6/8	17 1/8	20 7/8	21	135 1/8

COLUMBIA BLACKTAIL DEER
Odocoileus Hemionus Columbianus

Score	Length of Main Beam Right	Left	Inside Spread	Circumference at smallest place between burr & first point Right	Left	Number of Points Right	Left	Locality	Hunter	Date Killed	Rank
Minimum Score 120											
135	19	19 5/8	15 4/8	4 1/8	4 2/8	5	5	Humboldt County, CA	Edward F. Burgess	1965	138
135	18 6/8	18 6/8	15 6/8	4 3/8	4 2/8	5	5	Trinity County, CA	Andrew M. Felt	1986	138
135	22 6/8	23 2/8	20	4 4/8	4 3/8	4	4	Mendocino County, CA	Rodney E. Carley	1989	138
134 7/8	18 5/8	18 6/8	20 2/8	4 5/8	4 4/8	9	9	Mendocino County, CA	O.E. Schubert	1917	139
134 7/8	19 6/8	20 5/8	14 5/8	4 1/8	4 1/8	5	5	Mendocino County, CA	Jesse O. Foster	1964	139
134 7/8	22 3/8	22 2/8	18 3/8	4	4 2/8	4	5	Tehama County, CA	Mario Sereni, Jr.	1964	139
134 7/8	21 1/8	21 5/8	14 4/8	4 1/8	4 2/8	5	6	San Bernadino County, CA	James Tacke	1966	139
134 7/8	20 4/8	20 3/8	17 7/8	4 1/8	4 2/8	5	5	Siskiyou County, CA	George L. Wilson	1991	139
134 7/8	17 6/8	17 5/8	15 3/8	4	4	5	5	Mendocino County, CA	Bette C. Hill	1993	139
134 6/8	19 4/8	20	16 3/8	4 4/8	4 4/8	5	6	Trinity County, CA	Donald E. Stevens	1979	140
134 6/8	19 7/8	19 6/8	17 2/8	4 6/8	4 7/8	5	5	Humboldt County, CA	Bettie L. Lovie	1988	140
134 6/8	20 7/8	21	18 4/8	4 1/8	4 3/8	4	4	Trinity County, CA	Leon T. Gemini	1994	140
134 5/8	20 4/8	20 3/8	15 5/8	4 5/8	4 6/8	5	5	Siskiyou County, CA	Roy Eastlick	1965	141
134 4/8	21 1/8	21 2/8	20 2/8	4 1/8	4 3/8	7	6	Trinity County, CA	William M. Longhurst	1951	142
134 4/8	19 4/8	20	17	4 4/8	4 2/8	5	5	Humboldt County, CA	J.A. Phelps	1966	142
134 4/8	22	21 4/8	18 4/8	5 2/8	5 1/8	5	4	Sonoma County, CA	Richard O'Farrell	1984	142
134 3/8	22 5/8	21 2/8	22 3/8	4 7/8	4 7/8	5	4	Tehama County, CA	Bob C. Haase	1987	143
134 3/8	21 1/8	21 6/8	17 7/8	4 2/8	4 1/8	5	5	Humboldt County, CA	Christopher L. Rudd	1991	143
134 2/8	19 3/8	19 6/8	20 2/8	4 7/8	4 6/8	6	5	Mendocino County, CA	Sebastian D. Carrasco	1986	144
134 2/8	19 4/8	21	16	4	4 3/8	4	4	Humboldt County, CA	G.L. Dorris	1973	144
134 2/8	24 1/8	23 6/8	22 4/8	4 3/8	4 4/8	4	4	Colusa County, CA	Gregory R. Bonetti	1983	144
134 2/8	18 4/8	19 4/8	13	4 5/8	4 2/8	5	5	Mendocino County, CA	Gary D. Powell	1990	144
134 1/8	19 5/8	20	16 5/8	4 4/8	4 4/8	5	5	Mendocino County, CA	Danny Pardini	1976	145

Rank	Score	Length R	Length L	Inside Spread	Circ.	Circ.	Pts. R	Pts. L	Locality	Hunter	Date
145	134 1/8	18 2/8	18 2/8	14 7/8	4	4	6	5	Trinity County, CA	David Deininger	1980
146	134	19 6/8	19 2/8	16 2/8	3 6/8	3 4/8	7	5	Siskiyou County, CA	Alicia Whittaker	1970
146	134	18 4/8	19 3/8	17	4 6/8	4 6/8	5	5	Glenn County, CA	John Lohse	1994
147	133 7/8	20 4/8	21 3/8	13 5/8	3 6/8	3 5/8	5	5	Siskiyou County, CA	William E. Turner	1982
147	133 7/8	19 4/8	21 3/8	20	4 4/8	4 4/8	6	4	Contra Costa County, CA	Howard E. Gardner	1992
148	133 6/8	21 2/8	21 1/8	16	3 7/8	4	5	5	Mendocino County, CA	Terence K. Prechter	1986
148	133 6/8	21 2/8	21 5/8	17 2/8	4 3/8	4 3/8	5	4	Mendocino County, CA	Marvin DeAngelis	1978
148	133 6/8	21 2/8	21 1/8	16	3 7/8	4	5	5	Mendocino County, CA	Terence K. Prechter	1986
149	133 5/8	19 1/8	18 3/8	15 7/8	3 4/8	3 7/8	6	4	Siskiyou County, CA	Edwin W. Masonheimer	1978
149	133 5/8	21 3/8	21 2/8	21 5/8	4 4/8	4 3/8	4	4	Shasta County, CA	Mitchell A. Thorson	1992
150	133 4/8	21	22 4/8	17 4/8	4 6/8	5	6	5	Trinity County, CA	Barry Griffin	1976
150	133 4/8	22	20 4/8	20 4/8	4 6/8	4 4/8	5	6	Trinity County, CA	George M. Moxon	1977
150	133 4/8	22 1/8	22 1/8	18 1/8	4 6/8	4 6/8	7	6	Mendocino County, CA	Ryan McDonald	1991
151	133 3/8	18 3/8	18 3/8	17 3/8	4 4/8	4 4/8	5	5	Mendocino County, CA	Richard L. Moore	1989
151	133 3/8	20 2/8	20 3/8	19 3/8	4 1/8	4	4	4	Trinity County, CA	Reuben R. Tipton III	1993
151	133 2/8	19 1/8	18 5/8	16	3 2/8	3 2/8	5	4	Trinity County, CA	Kirk Finch	1975
152	133 2/8	20 7/8	20 2/8	17	4 2/8	4 2/8	5	5	Trinity County, CA	Ralph L. Perry	1980
152	133 1/8	22	22 7/8	21 1/8	4 5/8	5	5	5	Trinity County, CA	Hugh A. Dow	1969
153	133	20 4/8		19 4/8	4 4/8	5	5	5	Napa County, CA	Fred C. Framsted	1966
154	133	18 4/8	19 1/8	18 6/8	4 3/8	4 6/8	4	4	Humboldt County, CA	George B. Stiglich	1988
154	132 7/8	21 4/8	20 6/8	19 1/8	4 2/8	4 3/8	5	5	Humboldt County, CA	Dennis R. Lake	1988
155	132 7/8	23 3/8	21 6/8	19 4/8	4 5/8	4 4/8	5	5	Tehama County, CA	Joe McBrayer	1981
155	132 7/8	19 3/8	19 1/8	16 5/8	4	4 3/8	6	6	Mendocino County, CA	Gregory C. Moore	1985
155	132 7/8	21 4/8	20 6/8	19 1/8	4 2/8	4 3/8	5	5	Humboldt County, CA	Dennis R. Lake	1988
155	132 7/8	22 5/8	21 1/8	17	3 2/8	3 2/8	5	5	Mendocino County, CA	John E. Coughlin	1988
155	132 7/8	18 3/8	19 7/8	21 4/8	4 2/8	4 2/8	4	5	Trinity County, CA	Jim D. Odom	1989
156	132 6/8	21 5/8	20 5/8	17 6/8	4 4/8	4 4/8	5	4	Siskiyou County, CA	Paul J. Bruno	1985
156	132 6/8	17 6/8	19 1/8	16 4/8	3 6/8	3 7/8	5	5	Tehama County, CA	Daniel E. Osborne	1956
156	132 6/8	21	19 5/8	18 6/8	4 4/8	4 4/8	5	5	Mendocino County, CA	Mason Geisinger	1967
156	132 6/8	22 6/8	22	21 6/8	4 6/8	4 6/8	5	5	Mendocino County, CA	Jay M. Gates III	1984

COLUMBIA BLACKTAIL DEER
Odocoileus Hemionus Columbianus

Score	Length of Main Beam Right	Left	Inside Spread	Circumference at smallest place between burr & first point Right	Left	Number of Points Right	Left	Locality	Hunter	Date Killed	Rank
Minimum Score 120											
132 6/8	20 5/8	21 5/8	17 6/8	4 4/8	4 4/8	5	5	Siskiyou County, CA	Paul J. Bruno	1985	156
132 6/8	19 6/8	20 1/8	11	4 2/8	4 5/8	5	5	Santa Clara County, CA	Ben Mazzone	1995	156
132 5/8	20 5/8	20 5/8	16 4/8	4	4	5	5	Sonoma County, CA	H. James Tonkin	1996	157
132 5/8	20 4/8	20 2/8	16 1/8	4 1/8	4 3/8	5	5	Siskiyou County, CA	Daniel A. Rich	1990	157
132 3/8	22 2/8	22	19	5 1/8	4 5/8	5	4	Trinity County, CA	David L. Matley	1981	158
132 3/8	18 7/8	19 7/8	18 1/8	4	4 1/8	5	5	Siskiyou County, CA	Lawrence F. Weckerle	1982	158
132 3/8	20 4/8	20 4/8	16 3/8	4 1/8	4 1/8	5	6	Mendocino County, CA	Richard L. Moore	1989	158
132 3/8	22 7/8	21 6/8	16 1/8	4 1/8	4	5	5	Siskiyou County, CA	Edward P. Reardon	1989	158
132 2/8	20	20	16 4/8	4 1/8	4 2/8	5	5	Mendocino County, CA	Richard L. Moore	1987	159
132 2/8	19 5/8	18 7/8	18 2/8	4 5/8	4 1/8	5	4	Mendocino County, CA	P.R. Borton	1971	159
132 2/8	21 3/8	19 3/8	14 6/8	4 6/8	4 1/8	5	4	Humboldt County, CA	Guy Hooper	1977	159
132 2/8	20	20	16 4/8	4 1/8	4 2/8	5	5	Mendocino County, CA	Richard L. Moore	1987	159
132 1/8	20 6/8	20 4/8	15 1/8	5 2/8	5 1/8	4	4	Trinity County, CA	R.C. Kauffman	1936	160
132 1/8	20 6/8	19 6/8	19 1/8	3 2/8	3 2/8	4	4	Mendocino County, CA	Fred E. Borton II	1971	160
132 1/8	20	19 4/8	18 1/8	4	4	5	5	Trinity County, CA	Ronald L. Schneider	1979	160
131 7/8	22 3/8	21 6/8	18 5/8	4 3/8	4 3/8	4	4	Santa Clara County, CA	Gary D. Thompson	1994	161
131 6/8	19 1/8	19 3/8	14	4	3 7/8	5	5	Siskiyou County, CA	Sid E. Ziegler	1957	162
131 6/8	21	19 4/8	18	5	5	5	5	Trinity County, CA	Carter B. Dow	1961	162
131 6/8	19 1/8	18 5/8	14 4/8	4 2/8	4 2/8	5	5	Humboldt County, CA	Larry Wilson	1978	162
131 6/8	18 5/8	19 3/8	13 6/8	5 1/8	4 6/8	6	5	Trinity County, CA	Melvin M. Clair	1979	162
131 6/8	20 2/8	20	18 2/8	3 6/8	4	5	5	Trinity County, CA	Kenneth L. Cogle, Jr.	1981	162
131 6/8	20 4/8	20 4/8	21 3/8	4 4/8	4 3/8	5	5	Lake County, CA	Michael D. Keesee, Sr.	1982	162
131 4/8	19 6/8	19 1/8	17 2/8	3 6/8	3 6/8	5	6	Mendocino County, CA	James J. McBride	1982	163

Score								Locality	Name	Year	Rank
131 4/8	19 5/8	19 1/8	17 2/8	3 6/8	3 6/8	5	6	Mendocino County, CA	James J. McBride	1982	163
131 4/8	20 4/8	21 3/8	18 1/8	4 6/8	4 6/8	6	5	Trinity County, CA	Robert E. Fulmer	1993	163
131 2/8	19 6/8	19 6/8	17 4/8	3 7/8	4	5	5	Trinity County, CA	L. Irvin Barnhart	1986	164
131 2/8	19 6/8	19 6/8	17 4/8	3 7/8	4	5	5	Trinity County, CA	L. Irvin Barnhart	1986	164
131 2/8	21 1/8	19 4/8	18 4/8	3 7/8	3 7/8	5	5	Tehama County, CA	Richard D. Stillwell	1989	164
131 1/8	20 3/8	20	21 6/8	5 1/8	5 4/8	5	4	Mendocino County, CA	Richard L. Valladao	1991	165
131 1/8	20 7/8	21 5/8	23 4/8	4 2/8	4	5	5	Colusa County, CA	Walter Wright	1940	165
131	18 4/8	17 4/8	15 6/8	4	3 7/8	5	5	Siskiyou County, CA	George Quigley	1971	166
131	18 2/8	18 4/8	18 4/8	4 2/8	4 2/8	5	5	Siskiyou County, CA	Ramond Whittaker	1981	166
131	21 4/8	21 7/8	21 4/8	5 7/8	6 1/8	8	6	Mendocino County, CA	Betty L. Gidding	1992	166
130 7/8	20 7/8	20 4/8	16 5/8	3 7/8	3 7/8	5	5	Tehama County, CA	James D. Fiske	1956	167
130 7/8	17 5/8	19 4/8	16 7/8	4 2/8	4	5	5	Mendocino County, CA	John W. McGehee	1989	167
130 6/8	21 6/8	21 4/8	19 4/8	4 2/8	4	8	6	Siskiyou County, CA	Larry E. Richey	1956	168
130 6/8	20 5/8	19	19	4	4 3/8	5	4	Mendocino County, CA	Tom Enberg	1970	168
130 5/8	18	20	17 1/8	5	5	6	6	Lake County, CA	Bernard Domries	1940	169
130 5/8	24 2/8	23 3/8	23 2/8	4 3/8	4 4/8	4	5	Siskiyou County, CA	Vernon Sutherlin	1961	169
130 5/8	18 5/8	17 3/8	15 5/8	4 1/8	4 1/8	5	5	Stanuislaus County, CA	Scott Wilkinson	1987	169
130 4/8	22 5/8	22 1/8	21 1/8	4 2/8	4 1/8	4	4	Trinity County, CA	Wayne Erikson	1985	170
130 4/8	21 6/8	21 7/8	18 6/8	5 2/8	4 2/8	5	3	Mendocino County, CA	Mitchell A. Thorson	1969	170
130 4/8	19	19 5/8	15 4/8	4 2/8	4 2/8	4	4	Santa Clara County, CA	William J. McGrath	1982	170
130 4/8	22 5/8	22 1/8	21 1/8	4 2/8	4 1/8	4	5	Trinity County, CA	Wayne Erickson	1985	170
130 4/8	21	21 1/8	19 4/8	4 1/8	3 6/8	5	5	Trinity County, CA	Robert T. Hammaker	1991	170
130 4/8	19	19 2/8	19 5/8	3 5/8	4 5/8	5	5	Humboldt County, CA	Jim Dervin	1992	170
130 3/8	18 3/8	18 1/8	16 1/8	4 3/8	4 2/8	5	5	Mendocino County, CA	Helen F. Ornbaum	1960	171
130 3/8	20	20	16 3/8	4	4	5	4	Siskiyou County, CA	John Carmichael	1970	171
130 2/8	19 6/8	19 4/8	17	4 4/8	4 4/8	4	5	Santa Clara County, CA	John J. Marino	1993	172
130 2/8	19 7/8	19 7/8	19	4 2/8	4 3/8	5	5	Paskenta, CA	Mike Kalfsbeek	1994	172
130 1/8	20 3/8	20 1/8	20 1/8	4 5/8	4 2/8	4	4	San Mateo County, CA	Dan Caughey III	1988	173
130 1/8	20 3/8	20 1/8	20 1/8	4 5/8	4 2/8	4	4	San Mateo County, CA	Dan Caughey III	1988	173
130 1/8	22 2/8	21 4/8	18 4/8	4 2/8	4 2/8	4	4	Stanuislaus County, CA	Gary Thompson		173

COLUMBIA BLACKTAIL DEER

Odocoileus Hemionus Columbianus

Score	Length of Main Beam		Inside Spread	Circumference at smallest place between burr & first point		Number of Points		Locality	Hunter	Date Killed	Rank
	Right	Left		Right	Left	Right	Left				

Minimum Score 120

Score	Length of Main Beam Right	Left	Inside Spread	Circ. Right	Left	Points Right	Left	Locality	Hunter	Date Killed	Rank
130	22 1/8	22 2/8	15 6/8	3 5/8	3 5/8	5	3	Trinity County, CA	Terry H. Walker	1979	174
130	22 1/8	22 2/8	15 6/8	3 5/8	3 5/8	5	3	Trinity County, CA	Terry H. Walker	1979	174
130	20 2/8	19 6/8	19 2/8	4 3/8	4 4/8	5	5	Mendocino County, CA	Matt D. Mazzuca	1994	174
129 5/8	19 6/8	20 2/8	18 3/8	4	3 6/8	5	5	Trinity County, CA	John P. Livingston	1991	175
129 2/8	20 2/8	20 2/8	15 6/8	3 7/8	3 7/8	4	4	Trinity County, CA	Bob Gribble	1996	176
129 2/8	20 1/8	19 3/8	16 4/8	3 6/8	3 5/8	7	5	Trinity County, CA	Darold Adams	1951	176
129	20	17 5/8	14 4/8	3 7/8	4 7/8	4	5	Humboldt County, CA	Stephen Walker	1961	177
128 6/8	21 6/8	19 7/8	20	4 5/8	4 2/8	4	4	Stanuislaus County, CA	Jerry A. Wilkinson	1991	178
128 4/8	20	20 2/8	18 7/8	4 1/8	4 1/8	5	6	Trinity County, CA	Tony Stoer	1979	179
128 4/8	20 3/8	20 5/8	17 2/8	4 2/8	4 3/8	5	5	Stanuislaus County, CA	Jerry A. Wilkinson	1985	179
128 2/8	17 6/8	17 4/8	17 4/8	4	4	6	7	Santa Clara County, CA	Leon Gridder	1985	180
128 2/8	20	19 3/8	15 2/8	4 2/8	4 4/8	5	5	Trinity County, CA	Terry L. Barns	1991	180
128 1/8	21 2/8	22	19 5/8	4 4/8	4 4/8	5	4	Stanuislaus County, CA	Jerry A. Wilkinson	1986	181
127 7/8	20 4/8	21 2/8	15 3/8	3 3/8	3 3/8	4	4	Trinity County, CA	Marlene L. Coats	1988	182
127 2/8	21	21 3/8	21	4 4/8	4 4/8	4	5	Mendocino County, CA	Timothy Hickam	1991	183
126 5/8	18 1/8	19 1/8	20 1/8	4	4	5	5	Sonoma County, CA	William E. Soekland	1981	184
125 6/8	21 2/8	20 6/8	15	4 5/8	4 5/8	3	4	Mendocino County, CA	Tim Fowler	1992	185
125 6/8	19 4/8	19 4/8	19 2/8	4	3 7/8	5	5	Mendocino County, CA	Jon McQueen	1993	185
125 5/8	18 2/8	19 5/8	22 5/8	3 6/8	3 5/8	4	4	Humboldt County, CA	Lodewijk J. Wurfbain	1986	186
125 5/8	18 2/8	19 5/8	22 5/8	3 6/8	3 3/8	4	4	Humboldt County, CA	Lodewijk J. Wurfbain	1986	186
125 3/8	19 7/8	20 4/8	15 3/8	4 1/8	4 1/8	4	4	Humboldt County, CA	Michael Williams	1993	187
125 3/8	18 2/8	18 4/8	15 4/8	4 1/8	4 1/8	5	5	Santa Clara County, CA	Harry Marx	1990	187
125 2/8	19 4/8	19 6/8	16 4/8	3 6/8	3 7/8	5	5	Humboldt County, CA	Dan Noga	1991	188

Score								Locality	Hunter	Date	Rank
125	19 4/8	19 3/8	17	4 1/8	4	4	5	Sonoma County, CA	Matthew R. Petersen	1993	189
124 4/8	19 2/8	18	17 2/8	3 6/8	3 7/8	6	5	Santa Clara County, CA	Harry Marx	1991	190
124 4/8	22	19 4/8	15	3 7/8	4	4	4	Clear Lake, CA	Ronald May	1978	190
124 2/8	19 3/8	20 7/8	18	4	4	5	4	Santa Clara County, CA	Warren D. Huber	1971	191
124	18 5/8	18 4/8	16 2/8	5 2/8	5 2/8	4	4	Santa Clara County, CA	Ronald G. Duffey	1994	192
124	20 5/8	21 1/8	20 6/8	5 2/8	5 2/8	4	5	S. San Jose, CA	Danny Milovina	1996	192
123 6/8	21 5/8	20 2/8	18	3 5/8	4 2/8	3	4	Trinity County, CA	Joseph C. Cordonier	1991	193
123 5/8	18	18 1/8	15 5/8	4 3/8	4 2/8	5	5	Trinity County, CA	Monte D. Matheson	1988	194
123 4/8	21 2/8	20 2/8	16 5/8	3 7/8	3 7/8	6	5	Trinity County, CA	Brad Criner	1998	195
123 3/8	18 7/8	17 4/8	19 6/8	4 3/8	4 2/8	5	5	Mendocino County, CA	Timothy Hickam	1990	196
123	19 6/8	18 5/8	10	4 4/8	4 4/8	4	4	Santa Cruz County, CA	Homer Trumbo	1930	197
122 6/8	21 7/8	19 6/8	16	4 4/8	4 4/8	4	5	San Mateo County, CA	Daniel R. Caughey, Jr.	1964	198
122 6/8	21 7/8	19 6/8	16	4 4/8	4 4/8	4	5	San Mateo County, CA	Daniel R. Caughey, Jr	1964	198
122 3/8	19 4/8	21	16 1/8	4 3/8	4 1/8	4	4	San Mateo County, CA	Daniel R. Caughey, Jr.	1986	199
122 3/8	19 4/8	21	16 1/8	4 3/8	4 1/8	4	4	San Mateo County, CA	Daniel R. Caughey, Jr	1986	199
122 2/8	19	20	15 4/8	4 4/8	4 1/8	5	5	Humboldt County, CA	Don L. Corley	1982	200
122 2/8	19	18 5/8	17	4 2/8	5	5	4	Sonoma County, CA	Richard O'Farrell	1983	200
122 1/8	20 2/8	19 6/8	17 7/8	4	4	4	4	Trinity County, CA	Terry H. Walker	1976	201
122 1/8	20 2/8	19 6/8	17 7/8	4	4	4	4	Trinity County, CA	Terry H. Walker	1976	201
121 3/8	23 4/8	23 1/8	15 7/8	4 2/8	4 2/8	4	4	Mendocino County, CA	Donald W. Biggs	1993	202
121	18 6/8	18 6/8	18 6/8	4	4	4	4	San Mateo County, CA	Daniel R. Caughey, Jr.	1971	203
121	18 6/8	18 6/8	18 6/8	4	4	4	4	San Mateo County, CA	Daniel R. Caughey, Jr	1971	203
120 6/8	17 6/8	18 1/8	17 2/8	4 4/8	4 4/8	5	5	Trinity County, CA	Monte D. Matheson	1988	204
120 5/8	18 7/8	18 7/8	15	4 2/8	4 3/8	5	4	Santa Clara County, CA	Len Payne	1963	205
120 5/8	19 1/8	18 4/8	17 7/8	4	4	5	5	Trinity County, CA	Roger Baker	1993	205
120 5/8	20	20 2/8	19 3/8	4 4/8	4 2/8	4	5	Merced County, CA	Bill Gilardi	1988	205
120 4/8	18 3/8	18 7/8	16 6/8	4 4/8	4 6/8	5	5	Trinity County, CA	Jim Tonkin	1996	206

Blacktail

By Jerry Wilkinson

In 1986 the last week of Blacktail Deer season finally arrived much to my delight. The third week of September is the start of the rutting season and historically the big mature bucks appear that have been hiding all season.

My son and I hunt in the southwest area of Stanislaus County in zone 4. A good buddy of ours, Bill Martin, who is my neighbor near my home on the Monterey Peninsula always comes into the ranch the last week to have a couple of adult beverages with us and turn the steaks.

On Wednesday, mid morning, I was glassing a deep wide canyon named Buzzard. I had been glassing for about 15 minutes when all of a sudden, I spotted a big buck bedded down in the grass on the edge of a very large area of tall Chamise brush. The buck was about 800 yards away so I retrieved my spotting scope from the jeep and focused on the deer. His antlers were wide and I could count 4 points on one side.

The sun was going to be an issue soon and cause the buck to move, so I had to make a plan pronto. I decided to slide down into the canyon and try to move closer. After about 30 minutes I thought I could ease up to higher ground and look at the possibility of getting a shot. When I looked, the bed was empty and the buck was gone.

Back at camp at the B.B.Q. pit much conversation was directed to how I could get another chance at this big old boy.

The next morning I went back to the same look out and Scott was about a half mile north on the rim of Buzzard Canyon. It was hard to believe, because it is rare to see the same blacktail twice in a row, but there he was in all his splendor. A new plan was formulated in my nogan and I decided to try to get down wind from him and slowly work my way through the Chamise. After a miserable journey, I finally emerged from the brush missing a cap and scratched. The bed was again empty but I caught a glimpse of the buck heading north towards Scott. I followed in hot pursuit and even though he was getting further and further, I got to glass him. I could see he had a huge body and was 4x3. It looked like the buck disappeared into a different country that is difficult to hunt and I thought I probably wouldn't see him again.

Back at the ranch house, Scott told me he got a good look at him at long range and I better keep after the deer because he was a big one. I was tired and beat up and grumbling that I would give a bunch to have the big buck on my wall. Bill Martin fixed me a high ball and asked what would I give to get him, and I replied that if I ever bagged him, I would give Bill and his girlfriend Punky, 2 of my season tickets to the National Final Rodeo in Las Vegas. Heck, I'll even give you the airline tickets to get there.

On Friday, Bill had to go back to the Monterey Peninsula but before he left he told Scott that he was sure his dad would not give up. When your pop is dressing the big old boy out, remind him of his bet. I hunted elsewhere on Friday and pretty much had given up on my attempt. About 4 a.m. on Saturday morning I woke up and something told me to try again. I got a flashlight and coasted the jeep down to the creek so I wouldn't wake anyone up when I started it. I drove to the top of Buzzard Canyon and slipped down into an area near where the buck's bed had been. My blind was at the base of a boulder pile about 30 feet high. The wind was in my favor and I anxiously waited for daylight. When it got light I could see that the bed was empty. About 7 a.m. I determined it was all over. Why, I do not know, but I decided to climb up to the top of the rocks and look behind me into the chamise brush. To my astonishment, there he was in a small yellow grass clearing feeding about 200 yards uphill!

I suddenly discovered that I had left my rifle and field glasses at the base of the rocks, so I climbed down, retrieved my musket and scaled up to the top. The buck was broadside and entering the brushy jungle. I quickly put the cross hairs on his billboard a 30-06 150-grain was on its way. The buck disappeared into the brush and my access to where I last saw him was through 7-foot high brush. I waited a few minutes and decided the best pursuit was patience.

I hiked back to the jeep and headed for the ranch house to get Scott and my Rat Terrier and world champion deer dog, Trigger Wilkinson. As I crossed the Orestimba Creek I blasted the horn and Scott came out to the porch. I hollered, get Trigger, your rifle and let's go!

Back at Buzzard Canyon we decided to have Scott get on top of the rocks where I had shot, because from that vantage point, the other side of the chamise was visible and if I hit the buck and he was crippled, Scott could see him and get a shot.

I took my buddy, Trigger, put a leash on him and made my way to the yellow clearing where I last saw the buck. When I got to the 40 foot by 60 foot clearing, much to my disappointment, no blood was discovered. I started into the brush with Trigger ahead of me when Trigger became ballistic. I released the leash and in a second all hell broke loose! If a D8 bulldozer were operating ahead of me it would not have made as much noise or dust. All of a sudden I heard the blast from Scott's gun, then another and a third. "I got him" was finally echoing in the Canyon.

I advanced forward into the Chamise and came upon a huge pool of lung blood where the buck had laid down. I hiked down the canyon and met Scott and Trigger at the buck. I asked Scott "why didn't you shoot sooner?", and he laughed and replied, "I couldn't Trigger had a death grip on his backside". Scott was rather quiet and because the buck was moving so fast, I knew he thought that he had hit the buck twice and I had missed. I said nothing and took the first leg of packing the buck back to the jeep. When I put the buck down and before it was Scott's turn, I said, come with me, I want to show you something. When Scott saw that his old man did indeed hit the buck, he was definitely relieved and happy. The buck's antlers were heavy horned, 4x3 with two eye guards and 23 3/8 inches wide. When I look at the big old boy on my wall in the den, I wonder what Bill Martin thought about as he smiled and looked out the window of the airplane on his voyage to the National Final Rodeo?

PRONGHORN ANTELOPE

Pronghorn Antelope
Number One
Score: 89
Locality: Lassen Co.
Date: 1985
Hunter: Pick Up

PRONGHORN

Antilocapra Americana Related and Subspecies

Score	Length of Horn Right	Left	Circumference of Base Right	Left	Circumference at Third Quarter Right	Left	Inside Spread	Tip to Tip Spread	Length of Prong Right	Left	Locality	Hunter	Date Killed	Rank
Minimum Score 78														
89	17	16 3/8	7 2/8	7 1/8	3	3 1/8	11	5 2/8	6 5/8	6 5/8	Lassen County, CA	Pick up	1985	1
87 4/8	16	17 4/8	7 1/8	7	4 7/8	3 4/8	11 2/8	12	6	6 4/8	Modoc County, CA	Lynru M. Greene	1971	2
87 4/8	17 2/8	17 2/8	6 3/8	6 3/8	2 6/8	2 6/8	9 4/8	2 4/8	6 5/8	6 5/8	Modoc County, CA	Ron L. Reasor	1979	2
86	16	15 6/8	7	6 6/8	3 1/8	3	13 4/8	10 6/8	6 1/8	6 2/8	Lassen County, CA	David A. Tye	1987	3
85 4/8	16	16	6 6/8	6 6/8	3 1/8	3 3/8	8 4/8	3 7/8	6 1/8	6	Lassen County, CA	Jeff R. Rogers	1990	4
84 6/8	15 7/8	16 1/8	7 3/8	7 3/8	2 3/8	2 4/8	7	1	6 2/8	5 6/8	Modoc County, CA	William A. Shaw	1942	5
84 6/8	16 5/8	17	6 2/8	6 2/8	2 3/8	2 3/8	10 4/8	5 1/8	6 5/8	6 5/8	Modoc County, CA	Leland C. Lehman	1969	5
84 6/8	16 6/8	16 5/8	6 1/8	6 1/8	2 5/8	2 6/8	9 7/8	5	6 3/8	6 1/8	Modoc County, CA	Ernest Anacleto	1980	5
84 6/8	16 4/8	16 5/8	6 4/8	6 4/8	2 5/8	2 5/8	11 1/8	6 3/8	6 3/8	7 1/8	Lassen County, CA	Gary Caraccioli	1990	5
84 4/8	17 1/8	16 6/8	6 2/8	6 3/8	2 3/8	2 2/8	15 6/8	13 7/8	6 3/8	6 7/8	Modoc County, CA	J. Bob Johnson	1978	6
84 2/8	15 4/8	15 5/8	7 1/8	7	2 7/8	2 7/8	9	9 6/8	4 6/8	4 5/8	Modoc County, CA	Unknown	PR 1978	7
84 2/8	15 5/8	16 1/8	6 2/8	6 2/8	2 7/8	3 1/8	9 1/8	5 2/8	6 2/8	6 7/8	Modoc County, CA	Larry A. Owens, Sr.	1981	7
84 2/8	13 7/8	13 5/8	7 1/8	7 2/8	2 5/8	2 4/8	12 2/8	10 1/8	7 3/8	7 3/8	Lassen County, CA	Delbert W. Case	1992	7
84 2/8	17 3/8	17	6 2/8	6 2/8	2 4/8	2 4/8	9 3/8	3 2/8	6 6/8	6 4/8	Modoc County, CA	Don Perrien	1994	7
84	16 3/8	16 1/8	6 7/8	6 6/8	2 5/8	2 4/8	11	5 4/8	6	6	Lassen County, CA	Al J. Accurso, Jr.	1986	8
84	14 7/8	15 6/8	7	6 7/8	2 3/8	2 4/8	13 1/8	10 2/8	7 4/8	7	Lassen County, CA	Laery R. Brower	1990	8
83 6/8	16 6/8	16 6/8	6 4/8	6 1/8	2 6/8	2 6/8	7 1/8	2	6 4/8	6 4/8	Modoc County, CA	William B. Steig	1977	9
83 4/8	15 6/8	15 6/8	7 1/8	7	2 5/8	2 4/8	11 5/8	7 6/8	6 3/8	6 1/8	Lassen County, CA	Jason W. Langslet	1994	10
83 2/8	14 2/8	14 6/8	6 6/8	6 6/8	2 6/8	2 7/8	10 5/8	5 5/8	7 2/8	7	Modoc County, CA	David T. Eveland	1990	11
83 2/8	15 5/8	15 3/8	6 3/8	6 3/8	2 4/8	2 3/8	12 1/8	11 5/8	6 6/8	6 4/8	Lassen County, CA	Timothy L. Hartin	1992	11
83	16 5/8	16 6/8	6 4/8	6 2/8	2 6/8	2 7/8	11 7/8	7 7/8	5 2/8	5	Modoc County, CA	Richard Bishop	1986	12
82 6/8	16 3/8	16	6 2/8	6 2/8	2 7/8	3 2/8	13	7 4/8	6	5 2/8	Modoc County, CA	Dennis McClelland	1977	13
82 6/8	16	15 7/8	6 4/8	6 4/8	2 5/8	2 3/8	10 5/8	7 6/8	7	6 5/8	Modoc County, CA	Mary L. Crabtree	1992	13

											Location	Hunter	Year	Rank
82 6/8	16 6/8	16 6/8	6 5/8	6 5/8	2 3/8	2 4/8	14 1/8	10 6/8	5 6/8	5 6/8	Modoc County, CA	Kevin D. Fabig	1992	13
82 4/8	17 1/8	17	6 1/8	6	2 2/8	2 2/8	8	3 1/8	6	6	California	Bill Foster	1930	14
82 4/8	15 3/8	15 3/8	6 4/8	6 3/8	2 5/8	2 4/8	13 5/8	10 4/8	6 3/8	7	Lassen County, CA	Brad L. Ayotte	1977	14
82 4/8	15 4/8	15 2/8	6 6/8	6 5/8	2 5/8	2 4/8	12 2/8	7 1/8	5 5/8	5 6/8	Modoc County, CA	Mark Hansen	1978	14
82 4/8	16 2/8	16 3/8	7	6 7/8	2 3/8	2 4/8	8 1/8	6 2/8	5 5/8	5 3/8	Siskiyou County, CA	Rodney F. Royer	1979	14
82 4/8	16 4/8	16 6/8	6 5/8	6 3/8	3 1/8	3 2/8	12 1/8	7	4 7/8	4 7/8	Lassen County, CA	Bob Freed	1985	14
82 2/8	15 6/8	16	6 1/8	6 1/8	2 4/8	2 4/8	12 4/8	9	6 4/8	7	Lassen County, CA	Del S. Oliver	1978	15
82 2/8	17 3/8	16 7/8	6 2/8	6	2 4/8	2 2/8	11 7/8	9 4/8	6 2/8	5 5/8	Siskiyou County, CA	Laird E. Marshall	1984	15
82 2/8	18 7/8	19 4/8	5 6/8	5 6/8	2 3/8	2 3/8	17 7/8	15 4/8	4 5/8	4 5/8	Modoc County, CA	Rod Eisenbeis	1991	15
82	16 1/8	16 1/8	6 5/8	6 4/8	2 6/8	2 6/8	12 6/8	7 3/8	5 5/8	5 5/8	Lassen County, CA	Robert D. Luna, Jr.	1979	16
82	15 3/8	15 4/8	6 5/8	6 3/8	2 4/8	2 4/8	12	8 6/8	4 5/8	4 3/8	Lassen County, CA	Tommy B. Esperance	1991	16
82	15 4/8	15	7 2/8	7 3/8	2 7/8	2 7/8	10 6/8	7 3/8	4 6/8	4 3/8	Lassen County, CA	Joseph D. Nolan	1991	16

PRONGHORN ANTELOPE

By George Conant

In the summer of 1985 I received a phone call from a good friend of mine who worked for the CHP. He said that a car had hit a large buck antelope on Hwy 395 a little north of Hallelujah Jct. He asked if I wanted to go out with him and look for it. The driver of the car that hit it said the animal was not killed, but that it had hobbled off to the west of the highway. We looked for several days but found nothing. We decided to give it one more try, and that time I went to the other side of the highway just to look over some new country. It was not long before I found the antelope about 50 yards from the road. The cape was ruined by then, but I was able to save the horns, and have them mounted by Mike Boyce of Reno, Nevada. He did a beautiful job of mounting it.

By Don Perrien

Finally, after 15 years of applying for a California Antelope Permit, I received my 1994 tag. It was designated for Zone 3, Likely Tables.

Joining me for my pre-season scouting and hunting were my father, Earl and my friend, Scott Hushbeck. It was early in the morning on opening day, when I began my 45 minute belly crawling stalk just to get a 400 yd. shot. With a broad side standing target, I was able to hit the buck just before he was about to run off toward a large grass flat.

His horns are 17 3/8 long with 6 6/8 prongs and 6 4/8 bases for an official Boone and Crockett score of a 84 2/8 net. We had an excellent hunt on public land by spotting over 200 antelope with over 6 bucks sizing up to at least 15 inches.

The rifle I used was a Winchester Mod. 70 .243 Varmint with a Leopould Scope, and 100 gr. Hornady BTSP Handloads.

When it was over, my only disappointment was that after waiting 15 years, the entire hunt took less than 2 hours. However, with such a great animal, I surely can't complain.

DESERT SHEEP

DESERT SHEEP

Number One
Score: 187
Locality: California.
Date: 1970
Hunter: Picked Up

Number Two
Score: 184
Locality: Santa Rosa Mountains
Date: 1955
Hunter: Picked Up

Number Three
Score: 182 $^4/_8$
Locality: Riverside Co.
Date: 1963
Hunter: Picked Up

DESERT SHEEP

Ovis Canadensis Nelsoni

Score	Length of Horn		Circumference of Base		Circumference at Third Quarter		Greatest Spread	Tip to Tip Spread	Locality	Hunter	Date Killed	Rank
	Right	Left	Right	Left	Right	Left						
187	41 4/8	42 4/8	15 4/8	15 6/8	9 6/8	9 2/8	28	28	California	Picked up	1970	1
184	40 1/8	38 7/8	14 6/8	14 6/8	10 1/8	9 7/8	25 4/8	25 4/8	Santa Rosa Mts, CA	Picked up	1955	2
182 4/8	37	37 4/8	14 7/8	15 2/8	10	10 2/8	22 3/8	21 3/8	Riverside County, CA	Picked up	1963	3
182 2/8	37 7/8	37 1/8	16	16	9 1/8	9 2/8	24 1/8	23 5/8	San Gorgonio Wilderness, CA	John Bauder	1999	4
176 6/8	36 3/8	36 1/8	14 1/8	13 6/8	10 5/8	10 7/8	23 3/8	23 3/8	Santa Rosa Mts, CA	Picked up	PR 1958	5
175 6/8	35 5/8	36 1/8	14 1/8	14	10 2/8	10 4/8	21 2/8	17 5/8	San Diego County, CA	Picked up	1951	6
175 2/8	36 1/8	37 3/8	15 6/8	15 6/8	7 7/8	8 4/8	23 4/8	21 2/8	Riverside County, CA	David E. Combs	1996	7
175 1/8	37 1/8	40	13 7/8	13 7/8	8 6/8	9 3/8	20 5/8	22 6/8	Riverside County, CA	Picked up	PR 1967	8
175 1/8	34 2/8	34 7/8	15 2/8	15 2/8	10 5/8	10 1/8	21 6/8	20	San Bernardino County, CA	Arthur D. Bailey	1993	8
174 6/8	39	38 4/8	14 6/8	15 2/8	9 5/8	8 7/8	22 1/8	0	Barstow, CA	Picked up	1941	9
173 7/8	36 5/8	37	13 1/8	13 4/8	10 2/8	10 4/8	22 2/8	19 3/8	Anza Borrego Desert, CA	Picked up	1971	10
173 4/8	33 7/8	35 7/8	14 4/8	14 3/8	10	10 5/8	20 5/8	17 7/8	San Bernardino County, CA	Jerry K. Chandler	1993	11
173 1/8	32 6/8	30 7/8	15 4/8	15 3/8	11	11 6/8	24 4/8	23	Tulelake, CA	Picked up	1968	12
172 5/8	40 3/8	38 6/8	13 3/8	12 6/8	8 6/8	8 2/8	26 5/8	26 5/8	White Mts, CA	Picked up	1978	13
172	33	36	15	15 4/8	9	8 4/8	30 2/8	30 2/8	Tulelake, CA	Picked up	1963	14
171 4/8	35 1/8	34 7/8	14	14	10 2/8	10	19 4/8	19 4/8	Bullion Mts, CA	Picked up	1950	15
171 4/8	35 4/8	35	14 4/8	14 4/8	10	10	21 4/8	21 4/8	San Bernardino County, CA	Leon A. Pimentel	1989	15
171 4/8	35 1/8	34 7/8	14	14	10 2/8	10	19 4/8	19 4/8	Bullion Mts, CA	Picked up	1950	15
170 6/8	33 3/8	35 1/8	14	14	9 5/8	10 2/8	23 1/8	23 1/8	San Bernardino County, CA	Picked up	1960	16
170 5/8	34	38 5/8	13 6/8	13 5/8	9 2/8	9 1/8	24 4/8	24 4/8	Death Valley, CA	Picked up	1955	17
169 6/8	37 2/8	37	13 6/8	14	9 1/8	9	20 7/8	18 4/8	San Bernardino County, CA	Charles E. Cook	1989	18
169 4/8	34 4/8	34 2/8	14 6/8	14 6/8	9 4/8	9 1/8	23 3/8	20 4/8	San Bernardino County, CA	Jefre R. Bugni	1989	19
169 2/8	34 5/8	34 7/8	14	13 7/8	9 6/8	9 7/8	21 2/8	21 2/8	White Mts, CA	Picked up	1951	20
168	34 3/8	34 1/8	14 3/8	14 4/8	9 2/8	9 1/8	22	20 6/8	San Bernardino County, CA	Charles L. Rensing	1992	21
168	35 6/8	27 2/8	13 3/8	13	9 5/8	9 5/8	22 1/8	17 3/8	San Bernardino County, CA	Ron Smith	1992	21
167 7/8	35 2/8	33 3/8	14	14 1/8	9 5/8	9 5/8	21 2/8	21 2/8	San Bernardino County, CA	Alfred Adams	1994	22

Desert Sheep
Number Four
Score: 182 ²/₈
Locality: San Gorgonia Wilderness
Date: 1999
Hunter: John Bauder

Bighorn Sheep – California State Record Ram

Written by Tammera Anderson
As told to by John Bauder

STATE RECORD BIGHORN SHEEP taken in the San Gorgonio Wilderness on February 6, 1999. John Bauder of Rancho Cucamonga harvested one of the largest nelsoni desert bighorn ram taken in the nation and the largest in California. The ram green scored 182 2/8 points on the Boone & Crockett scoring system, with 16 inch bases and 38+ inch horn length. The previous record was 178 1/8.

Who would have ever thought that when I received the only draw tag for the San Gorgonio Wilderness that a new state record would be harvested. I am still high from the excitement. Just beating the odds of receiving the tag was tremendous. Let me back up to the beginning. Opening the mail that day, I couldn't believe my eyes. Just like thousands of other hunters, I have been sending in my application to hunt bighorn sheep since the program had started. Just like thousands of other hunters, I was never lucky enough to draw a tag. Well, today was my lucky day! The San Gorgonio Wilderness is in my backyard. My hunting buddies and I have hunted deer for many years there and during these hunts I had seen bighorn sheep. This was so great, who should I call first?...

After making many phone calls to share the good news with my hunting friends, the wheels started in motion as to how to approach the hunt. Having hunted with a bow for the last 10 years or so, the desire to take a ram by bow was my first choice. My friend Gary Drewry is an avid bow hunter and jumped at the chance to help me as well as friend Mike Dennett. We all work in construction, so when my boss, Greg Stires, found out he was more than supportive. He's accomplished his "grand slam" and worked with me to get the time off to scout and hunt.

My mail was flooded with brochures from outfitters. All of them were from out of the state except for one. Greg had suggested that I hire a guide, but since my friends and I had hunted the area a guide was out of the question. I spoke to anyone who knew the area, picking their brains about sheep history, location, and their patterns. There were so many directions and advice given to me, I just became confused.

All tag recipients must attend an orientation put on by the Department of Fish & Game. The day was more than I expected. All of us received maps of the area and information on hunting sheep such as what to look for, habitat & taxidermy. The San Gorgoino Wilderness Outfitters, was also helpful to me, providing a hunting aspect.

Gary, Mike, and myself decided to start scouting in the Mine Shaft area where we had seen sheep. Since we had yet to have any significant weather, it would seem that the animals would be up high. Wrong! We didn't see a thing. I called Jim Davis to get more guidance. He told me different areas where sheep had been seen.

Many of my weekends were spent pre-scouting prior to the start of the hunting season. Finally opening day arrived. The weather was hot and dry. The terrain with repetitive, steep canyons. Each trip I would bring both my rifle and bow. Everyone took turns carrying them. During one trip Mike, Travis (Mike's son), and myself spent a long, uncomfortable night's sleep on the side of a mountain. It was steep enough that we had to carve out a flat area to sleep on. On another trip it got so cold that water was frozen and the wind was howling. Getting into sheep country involved backpacking for long distances over rough terrain. This was just a taste of how tough the terrain is to hunt. Plus, there weren't any sheep in sight. I soon realized that harvesting a ram with a bow would most likely be impossible.

I called Terry Anderson. After speaking to him, he suggested I try a lower elevation to find sheep. He agreed to scout in-between his sheep hunts in the Orocopia's and the Old Dad Mountains. He also put us in contact with long time friends of his, Don and Helen Middleton. They live close to the train head of the Pacific Crest Trail. I thought this would be worth a try. Sure couldn't hurt. Especially since I hadn't had any luck thus far. One concern I had was that the trail head parking area is known for having your vehicle broken into and vandalized. However, Don offered to ride up with us to the trail head and bring my truck back to his place. He would then meet us at an appointed time.

Mike, Gary, and I didn't have any luck in this lower area. However, Terry spotted a group of four ram's and took some good video of two potential rams to harvest.

On Sunday the thirteenth day of hunting Mike, Gary, and myself spotted the group that Terry had seen. We couldn't get close to them. The rams seemed to know we were there and acted nervous. This was frustrating not being able to get near them. I unfortunately had to return to work and had made a commitment the following weekend. It worried me that by the time I would be able to return the sheep would have possibly moved on. Knowing that an opportunity could be missed. I got in touch with Terry on Wednesday. He had just completed a sheep hunt in the Old Dad Mountains. He arrived in camp with Mark Jones (Orocopia sheep tag hunter). All of us discussed the difficulty I was having getting close enough to the sheep. the next morning I officially signed on with him to guide for me.

All of us scouted the rams together that day. Within this group two rams stood out. Terry described the #1 ram with good length, mass, and symmetry. The #2 ram also had good symmetry and length, without the mass. The #1 ram definitely was a keeper. While watching them he said to me "You need to name the #1 ram". This was something I had never heard of. He told me that he names all of the significant and important rams. The #1 ram was given the name "Moses". This was because Terry hikes with a walking stick made from sororo cactus stalk, reminding me of Moses's staff.

Terry continued to watch the group for the next six days. The two rams I was interested in settled down during this time and never wandered more than a mile or two from where they were first sited.

Gary and I rejoined Terry at base camp in the evening of Wednesday, February 3, Thursday morning the weather changed to rain. All of us hiked up to where the ram's had bedded down. Gary was placed in a spotter position. Terry and I hiked farther up to glass.

Soon after daybreak a group of seven rams were spotted. They were coming off the mountain down to the bottom of the canyon. Just sure that they could see us, I signaled Terry to drop down to our bellys. The animal's seemed to be nervous and wary. Frequently staring in our direction, as if to see right through us. Moses was in this group. He seemed to be worried about something. The wind was in our favor and neither of us thought it was us. But, you never know!

It wasn't long before Moses took two smaller rams back up the mountain and out of site. My heart sunk! The #2 ram was in the other group and we didn't want to spook them off. We laid in the mud in a constant rain and watched them drink from the spring. For 2.5 hours we waited and watched as they nervously worked their way back up the mountain.

Moses was gone and when your in weather like this you start thinking "Just take a sheep, any sheep". So, with Terry's legs to support my gun out of the mud, I released the safety. My finger was on the trigger: the #2 ram in my site. Terry said "He's nice, but he's not Moses". The #2 ram wasn't what I wanted. Moses was my goal. We signaled to Gary to return to camp. We would look for Moses tomorrow.

Friday brought fog in the mountains. We could barely see our hands. This didn't let up from dark to dark. Mike re-joined us this day. That evening we studied the videos that Terry had taken the previous week. After talking for several hours a plan was agreed upon for Saturday. This was truly a group effort. Better weather was expected and the hope that the weather hadn't moved the sheep.

Saturday was cool and sunny. "What a beautiful day to shoot a sheep!" I said. Two days of bad weather had moved on. Hopefully, the rams had not. The four of us hiked up a ways together. It had been decided that Mike and Gary would climb high to a previously chosen spot. This would give them a good vantage point to signal Terry and myself. We stayed lower from where the rams had been seen two days prior and located them to the west of our position. Two rams were spotted, no Moses. A short time later five more rams came into view. Moses was in this group. He could be identified by his large body and horn mass. He stood out! Gary and Mike were signaled. The stock had started.

Believing that the rams were moving to higher ground we climbed the ridge opposite from them. This was an almost vertical climb. About half way up Terry and I stopped to assess the rams position. To our amazement, they were almost straight across the canyon from us feeding. Terry got out his Bushnell rangefinder. They were out of shooting range at four hundred yards. Unaware of us they continued to feed for about twenty minutes. Then abruptly they stopped and lined up single file with Moses in the lead. Where could they be going? Fortunately, they moved westward across a small ravine onto a ridge finger. This narrowed my position to 315 yards from Moses. Placing myself in a comfortable shooting position. I had loaded my 270 Winchester model 70 XTR: hand reload with 150gr Speer bullet. Set to shoot, I pulled the trigger, and misfired! It was so intense that it pulled my focus away for a minute. Ejecting the bullet, I started fumbling with it to see what had gone wrong. Terry grabbed the bullet and refocused me on the task at hand. Thankfully, Moses was still in position to get a good shot. The sheep remained unaware that we were even there. I repositioned myself and fired off a second shot. This time shooting over Moses at 315 yards. He moved out of site. I couldn't believe it. Now what?

The #2 ram was still within range. He was certainly beautiful. Just then, Moses reappeared over the ridge. What luck! Terry checked his range finder, 348 yards. With him in my cross hairs of my Redfield 3 x 9 scope, I fired! Terry was sure I hit him, I wasn't. We quickly counted. There were six rams where there had been seven. We were sure he had dropped in the canyon below. However, the longer the companion rams stood there the more unsure I became that he was hit. Twenty to thirty minutes went by before the group moved off.

We started to move toward the cliff that they had left. This was an incredibly steep and difficult climb. It took two hours to reach the area. Mike and Gary had previously lost visual contact of us. So they followed the sound of the shot.

When all of us converged at the site there wasn't any signs of blood. This only added to my fear that I hadn't hit him. Terry continued to be confident that I had. Looking closer at the place where we had seen him drop off, I saw fresh slide marks in the soft sand. As I followed the marks, there he was seventy to seventy five yards from where we stood! He had dropped under the thick brush. What an exciting and emotional moment!

I started climbing down to him. The closer I got the larger than life he became. Reaching him, I moved him from under the brush and saw that I had shot him in the center front chest area. A clean shot that exited through the left shoulder. Terry was watching through his video camera. He later told me that when he focused in on the ram he was amazed at the mass and length. The closest he had gotten to him while scouting was one to one and a half miles away. I was thrilled!

Pulling out a cloth sewing tape from my pack I measured the bases and length. He measured sixteen inch bases and thirty-eight inch length. Wow! I called Terry, Mike, and Gary down to me. Terry rough scored him and we knew we had a new state record. All of us were kids again! I was elated with the team effort to harvest an incredible ram. Moses was perfect. He only had a small "V" cut in the left horn. His coat was in great condition and an estimated weight of 225#. He seemed to have no major deductions. It was unbelievable that such a ram could exist. After all our hooping, hollering, and picture taking we did the necessary processing. We spent four hours packing out.

That evening at dinner we reflected on what it took to accomplish the harvest of such a great trophy animal. It is important to have great optics. These animals are difficult to get close to. Terry uses a Leica APO Televid 77 spotter scope. He takes most of his scouting video through it. This is on hunt that scouting is crucial to the success of the harvest. The ability to study an animal through video was definitely beneficial. This country demands you to be in the best possible shape.

This is one adventure that will be impossible to top. In the history of the California sheep program, a draw tag holder has never taken such a large ram as this. I have deepened my appreciation for the importance of having great hunting partners and a knowledgeable guide. It makes the harvest even greater when your wife is as supportive as mine is about my hunting. I have reaped the rewards from the work done by the California Department of Fish and Game. They have and continue to develop the sheep program through their research and proper management. The program continues due to contributors like Robert Petersen who has generously donated through the purchase of the auction tags. Associations such as FNAWS, California Deer Association, and the Society for the Conservation of Bighorn Sheep work continuously to raise funds, increase public awareness, enhance sheep habitat, and much more through membership and volunteers. I am and will be forever thrilled and appreciative for the opportunity to hunt.

FACTS: Year: 1999
　　　　Hunter: John Bauder
　　　　Location: San Gorgonio Wilderness
　　　　Species: Nelsoni desert bighorn sheep
　　　　Outfitter: San Gorgonio Wilderness Outfitters, Terry Anderson
　　　　Equipment: Winchester 270 model 70 XTR, hand reload with 150 gr. Speer bullets, Bogen tripod, Bushnell rangefinder
　　　　Optics: Redfield 3 x 9 scope, Leica APO Televid 77 spotter scope, 10 x 50 Bushnell Binoculars, 20 x 60 Bausch & Lomb spotter scope

Desert Sheep
Number Seven
Score: 175²/₈
Locality: Riverside County
Date: 1996
Hunter: David E. Combs

BLACK BEAR

BLACK BEAR

Number One
Score: 23 3/16
Locality: Mendocino Co.
Date: 1993
Hunter: Robert Shuttleworth, Jr.

Number Two
Score: 22 13/16
Locality: Ventura Co.
Hunter: Loren C. Nodolf

BLACK BEAR

Ursus Americanus

Score	Greatest Length of Skull without Lower Jaw	Greatest Width of Skull	Locality	Hunter	Date Killed	Rank
23 3/16	13 15/16	9 4/16	Mendocino County, CA	Robert J. Shuttleworth, Jr.	1993	1
22 13/16	14 1/16	8 12/16	Ventura County, CA	Loren C. Nodolf	1990	2
22 2/16	13 12/16	8 6/16	Kern County, CA	Danny R. Thomas	1988	3
22 2/16	13 6/16	8 12/16	Mendocino County, CA	Jay Bromley	1991	3
22 2/16	13 13/16	8 5/16	Mendocino County, CA	Chris Brennan	1995	3
22	13 10/16	8 6/16	Los Angeles County, CA	Joe L. Clay	1992	4
21 14/16	13 8/16	8 6/16	Santa Barbara County, CA	Donald Geivet	1999	5
21 12/16	13 2/16	8 10/16	Ventura County, CA	Joey La Salle	1992	6
21 12/16	13 2/16	8 10/16	Trinity County, CA	Blue Millsap	1994	6
21 11/16	13 5/16	8 6/16	Mendocino County, CA	E.J. Vamm	1928	7
21 11/16	13 5/16	8 6/16	Kern County, CA	George H. Hershberger	1985	7
21 11/16	13 5/16	8 6/16	Ventura County, CA	Marsha Vauhgn	1990	7
21 10/16	13	8 10/16	Mendocino County, CA	Andy Bowman	1930	8
21 10/16	13 2/16	8 8/16	Ventura County, CA	Chris Ames	1992	8
21 10/16	13 4/16	8 6/16	Glen County, CA	John H. Knight	1994	8
21 8/16	13 4/16	8 4/16	Ventura County, CA	James B. Wade	1977	9
21 7/16	13 2/16	8 5/16	Mariposa County, CA	Bert Palmberg	1957	10
21 7/16	13 1/16	8 6/16	Ventura County, CA	Mark Karluk	1996	10
21 6/16	13	8 6/16	Humboldt County, CA	Dean Early	1977	11
21 6/16	13 4/16	8 2/16	Mendocino County, CA	R. Larry Hyder	1991	11
21 6/16	13 1/16	8 5/16	Plumas County, CA	Monty D. McCormick	1992	11
21 6/16	12 14/16	8 8/16	Mendocino County, CA	Lawrence E. Taylor	1993	11
21 5/16	13 5/16	8	Coburn Lake, CA	Lauren A. Johnson	1960	12
21 5/16	13 3/16	8 2/16	Mendocino County, CA	Gene H. Whitney	1971	12
21 5/16	13 5/16	8	Santa Barbara County, CA	Picked Up	1982	12

BLACK BEAR
Uusus Americanus

Score	Greatest Length of Skull without Lower Jaw	Greatest Width of Skull	Locality	Hunter	Date Killed	Rank
21 5/16	13	8 5/16	Mendocino County, CA	John Jacobs	1985	12
21 5/16	13	8 5/16	San Benardino County, CA	Rahul T. Mathur	1995	12
21 4/16	13 6/16	7 14/16	Los Angeles County, CA	Picked Up	1952	13
21 4/16	13 7/16	7 13/16	Tehama County, CA	Jim Cox	1980	13
21 4/16	12 12/16	8 8/16	Mendocino County, CA	Miles Dupret	1984	13
21 4/16	13	8 4/16	Shasta County, CA	Richard L. Moore	1990	13
21 4/16	13 2/16	8 2/16	Mendocino County, CA	Steven W. Shelton	1993	13
21 3/16	12 11/16	8 8/16	Yolo County, CA	Walter D. Foster	1983	14
21 2/16	13 3/16	7 15/16	Los Angeles County, CA	Leo J. Reihsen	1961	15
21 2/16	13 2/16	8	Mammoth Mt., CA	Clarke Merrill	1963	15
21 2/16	13 5/16	7 13/16	Shasta County, CA	Ivan L. Marx	1965	15
21 2/16	13	8 2/16	Trinity County, CA	Picked Up	1967	15
21 2/16	13 2/16	8	Lake County, CA	David C. Sharp	1972	15
21 2/16	12 14/16	8 4/16	Humboldt County, CA	Conrad H. Will	1990	15
21 2/16	13 5/16	7 13/16	San Benardino County, CA	Rodney K. McGree	1993	15
21 1/16	13 7/16	7 10/16	Santa Barbara County, CA	Charles Tant	1940	16
21 1/16	13 2/16	7 15/16	Trinity County, CA	Dorrel K. Byrd	1994	16
21 1/16	12 13/16	8 4/16	Trinity County, CA	Curt M. Connor	1995	16
21	13 2/16	7 14/16	Santa Barbara County, CA	Picked Up	1984	17
21	12 14/16	8 2/16	Tuolumne County, CA	Stacy J. Willoughby	1994	17
21	12 15/16	8 1/16	Siskiyou County, CA	Terry Culbertson	1994	17
21	13 3/16	7 13/16	Humboldt County, CA	Jerry R. Caradoza	1996	17
20 13/16	13 5/16	7 8/16	Mendocino County, CA	Edward DeNatale	1994	18
20 12/16	12 11/16	8 1/16	Tulare County, CA	Jeffrey L. Davison	1992	19
20 11/16	12 11/16	8	Shasta County, CA	Kevin D. Sanders	1990	20

20 10/16	12 12/16	7 14/16	Mendocino County, CA	Joseph A. Cantaroni, Sr.	1982	21
20 8/16	12 13/16	7 10/16	Stonyford, CA	Brad Criner	2000	22
20 7/16	12 13/16	7 10/16	Lassen County, CA	Richard J. Retterath	1993	23
20 4/16	12 4/16	8	Trinity County, CA	Kenneth L. Van De Riet	1992	24
20 3/16	12 6/16	7 13/16	Tulare County, CA	J.J. McBride	1993	25

November Bruin

By Brad Criner

During the deer season I had spent some time hunting and noticed a lot of bear sign in a canyon. I thought later in bear season I would go take a look, and I did. Late in bear season I arrived in the early morning dark; I planned to hunt up this secret canyon of mine. When the darkness gave way to the light, I started slippin up this canyon being very quiet. With the wind in my face, I proceeded. Knowing this was an ideal condition, I stopped to glass the hillsides that drained into it.

While I was looking at the hillside, I saw a brown object under a large oak tree that just didn't look like a log. I threw up the glasses to see the large bruin feeding on acorns. I made my stalk with the right wind and the confidence of many hunts before this one. I was able to get to a large pile of rocks, take off my pack, and lay my 25-06 caliber across it. The bear was about 200 yards away feeding. I got a solid picture in my scope and sent the 120 grain Nosler partition on its way. With a dead on shoulder shot, the bear went down rolling down the hill into a large patch of juniper bushes.

When I got to the bear, I was amazed at his size. I started thinking that if I was going to shoot bears maybe I would need a bigger gun! The next question was: What does a 155 pound man do with a 550 pound bear? Call for help. I field dressed the bear and walked out to the truck and called the guys.

Mike, Domer, and Frenchy came up with Mike's new 450 Honda, that will never be the same. We were able to get the bear out after reloading it about a dozen times, with some interesting procedures. I drove home right through town with that bear straddling the 4 wheeler and getting some odd looks from the town folk. I headed straight for the game warden's house for validation. The bear weighed 550 pounds and measured 7'3" and it was a very exciting day!

TULE ELK

CALIFORNIA TULE ELK
(Cervus Nannodes)

Written by J. J. McBride

Stepping out of the tall tules, the large bull bugled his challenge to any other bull within earshot. Some distance away, a small group of cows milled about as the screaming bugle was noted by their herd bull. Dotting the wetlands near the Sacramento River, small herds of elk extended as far as the eye could see. The herd bull appeared nervous on hearing the airborne insult and moved cautiously forward. Some distance away, sights began to focus on the bull's neck. The large puff of white smoke and the thunderous roar of the shot caused many blackbirds to take to the air momentarily. The large elk crumpled as the cows took flight to a hidden part of the marsh. The hunter had his chores to do and soon the elk was loaded into his boat, destined for the demanding meat markets of the rapidly expanding town of San Francisco.

The vast areas of the Sacramento and San Joaquin Valleys were no more than an endless grassland, intersected by swamps and liberally dotted with various types of oak and willow. The solemn silence of this pristine scene had not yet been violated by the noise of the internal combustion engine and unending black asphalt trails were still 50 years away. The year was 1851.

The gentle rolling hills of the brushy Coastal range and grass valleys provided feed and protection for over 500,000 tule elk. Father Junipero Serra and other missionaries had constructed their missions a day's walk apart in this detached possession of Mexico. Small settlements survived on ranching or agrarian interests. Native Americans and Hispanics made up the bulk of the population and worked together to carve out an existence in this wilderness guarded on the East by the snow capped sierras. The fashionable populations of New York and other East Coast cities had no idea that sights such as Yosemite even existed.

The sun shone at it's apex and a man thought he saw something glitter in the stream bed below him in the American River. John Sutter's mill would be the beacon for the largest population invasion the future state would ever see. Gold fever caused men to drop everything, abandon families, and seek their unlimited fortunes in the far away land on the other side of the continent. Horse or ship were the only means of transportation of the shovel/pick ax army that came to explore the gold laden streams. Cities sprang up overnight as hoards descended to claim their wealth.

The demand for meat could not even come close to being met by the meager ranching industry. Few miners tasted success and others had to rely on their resourcefulness to survive. Some became market hunters to supply the incessant needs of the exploding population. The vast unlimited numbers of elk provided convenient targets for livelihood and occupation.

The present day area of Martinez, Livermore Valley, and the Sacramento Delta were reported to have in excess of 50,000 elk in the 1840's. Elk were commonly seen on many hills of the San Francisco Bay Area by sailors. Marin, Sonoma, Napa valleys harbored sizeable numbers as did the Santa Clara Valley to Monterey. In the San Jaoquin Valley, large concentrations were known to exist around Stockton and south to the Madera River, and even extended down to Buttonwillow in Kern Co.

When the 1849 Gold rush began, no prohibitions were in place and the annihilating slaughter began. The elk around the San Francisco Bay Area and the Sacramento Valley were the first to go to extinction. So huge were the numbers taken, that in 1852 the state legislature passed a law setting a six month season in 12 counties and later extended it to the entire state by 1854. In 1873, the legislature passed a law for total protection. However, by this time there was considerable doubt that any Tule elk still existed.

The old Habitat of the Tule elk was now divided by barbed wire, roads, fields, and farms. The miners had left for the silver strike in Nevada and those that chose not to go turned to the land. California was now a state and had embarked on a plan to develop agriculture in the lower San Jaoquin Valley. In the area of Buena Vista Lake, located midway between Taft and Bakersfield, a drainage canal was being dug on the Miller-Lux Ranch to provide irrigation for the arid land. From amongst the thick willows in the area emerged two pair of Tule elk.

These were the last four survivors that stood between total extinction. The elk were fiercely protected by Henry Miller, who tried to save them in 1875 by setting aside a special area for them. Twenty years later, the total number of Tule elk had increased to just under 30 head; they weren't extinct yet. Miller was the first steward of the Tule elk and his dedicated efforts were responsible for their existence. Untold damage to fences and crops by the elk were gladly absorbed and overlooked as the small herd began to grow and expand. With over 350 Tule elk roaming about his Buttonwillow ranch in 1904, Henry Miller turned the herd over to the U.S. Biological Survey to expand their range.

Throughout the next 15 years, various transplants were attempted with the total population over 500 head. Some of the different locales were Sequoia National Park, Yosemite National Park, and the Del Monte area near Pebble Beach. Due to the danger to the public by rut crazed bulls, the Del Monte herd was captured and relocated to Cache Creek area of Colusa County; and the Yosemite herd had a similar relocation to the Owens Valley. Both of these herds were moved onto private property initially, where the landowners accepted stewardship for the elk; whereas those animals that were just released on public land were soon gone from existence in a few years.

The Owens Valley area represents five different herd locations on the eastern slope of the Sierras. Each of these groups began to increase and there used to be hunts to keep the herd within its range carrying capacity, which was about 1200 animals. Hunters used to be accompanied by either a warden or biologist to ensure that only the proper animals were harvested. This program was in effect until 1971, when a lawsuit was filed demanding a closed season until the elk numbered 2000 as they were endangered.

In the mid 70's, to try to achieve this goal, the satellite herd concept was started. If a landowner had adequate property, which was found to contain suitable elk habitat, California fish & Game would transplant a small group of elk to the property. The landowner had to agree to make further improvements, such as special crop plantings and watering systems, etc., and after a period of five years, the landowner would be given tags to remove the surplus elk. This was the basis of the "580" program and is in effect on many ranches today. The landowners again have accepted the responsibility for the stewardship of the elk and guaranteed their future, for the season was opened in 1990 with more than 2000 head statewide.

Today there are over 35 different herds of Tule elk roaming a small portion of their original habitat and their numbers total more than 3600. In the period of the last 125 years, since the last 4 elk were located near Bakersfield, they have been saved from extinction. Their former habitat now comprises freeways, subdivisions, large agriculture holdings and ranches.

In 1997, the Boone and Crockett Club, the records keepers of North American Big Game, acknowledged the Tule elk as a separate species and opened their category. In order to qualify as a separate species, the animal has to be different than any known species, be separated by a physical or geographical boundary for purity and no inbreeding, and be recognized as a legal species to take under the local game laws. The first exhibit of the Tule elk class will be in Springfield MO in 2001.

The Tule elk differ in many ways from their cousins; the Rocky Mountain and the Roosevelt elk. Throughout its range, the tule appears as gray in the pelage as compared to the creamy yellow of the Rocky or light brown of the Roosevelt. Upon examining the feet, Rocky Mountain and Roosevelt elk appear very similar in they have rounded tracks like cattle. The Tule elk has pointed hooves with a raised outer edge. This trait is similar to the Sitatunga of Africa and dwells in the marshes.

The antlers of the Tule elk are uniquely different from the other elk. The Rocky Mountain elk normally have long main beams with 6 or more matched points to a side. Anything unmatched or not symmetrical is penalized. A bifurcated point is abnormal and also a deduction. The Roosevelt of the Pacific northwest have shorter, heavier beams and points and only have to be symmetrical to the 4th point (G4) and they receive credit for all crown points and point lengths past the G4. Some examples of Roosevelt have some palmation about the G4 and that can be normal.

The Tule elk antlers have a tendency in the larger bulls to exhibit bifurcated points, palmation, and crown points. Acknowledging these traits, the Roosevelt scoring system is the proper one to use on Tule elk. Tule elk have to be considered a "bottleneck" species in that they went from 500,000 down to 4 and back up to 3600 head. Over 50% of the bulls on their first point (G1) will display an upward projection where the point erupts from the main beam. This seems to be unique to the Tule and a small percentage show the point off both G1's.

Many have considered the Tule elk as the dwarf or diminutive member of the elk family. Their original habitat was grasslands and oak/oat hills. They were not known to frequent the pine or heavy timber ridges of other elk.

In 1990, when hunting was again opened, coveted public drawing tags were issued for Grizzly Island in the Suisun Marsh. As the bulls were harvested, Fish & Game personnel assisted the hunters in removing the animals whole. Surprisingly, many of the bulls were tipping the scales at close to 700 lbs. One bull in 1995 tipped the scales at 980 lbs.

One particular bull, transplanted to Grizzly Island in 1995 to freshen the gene pool, is of particular note. He was the offspring of one of the largest bulls known and was given the nick name of Son o' Stud. In June of 1995, he attempted to swim back to Grizzly Island from a nearby island and drowned. fish & Game was summoned by the Coast Guard because the floating carcass was a "navigational hazard". The Fish & Game personnel removed the head and submerged the remaining carcass. The massive antlers were taken to Yountville. The antlers had a gross score of 425 points with a net score of 403 (15 points larger than the world record Roosevelt elk). The head was mounted and was loaned out to various organizations for fund raisers. The Rocky Mt. Elk Foundation borrowed it and failed to secure it properly in an open truck. When the truck hit a bump, the head blew out of its crate and was smashed moments later by an 18 wheeler, thus destroying the World Record Tule elk.

There will never be 500,000 Tule elk again, but they are saved from extinction. They are the greatest comeback story of the last 150 years in game and today are a viable game animal with sustaining populations providing the sportsmen with the opportunity to savor this rare elk, only found in California.

The people of California owe an unpayable debt to Henry Miller and his fellow stewards for saving this magnificent animal.

Tule Elk
Number One
Score: 365
Locality: Solano County
Date: 1997
Hunter: Bryce Evans

TULE ELK
Cervus Elaphus

Score	Length of Main Beam Right	Left	Inside Spread	Circumference at smallest place between first & second points Right	Left	Number of Points Right	Left	Locality	Hunter	Date Killed	Rank
Minimum Score 245											
351	48 6/8	47 4/8	51 3/8	7 1/8	6 4/8	9	9	Solano County, CA	Quentin Hughes	1997	1
346 6/8	48	49 4/8	37 4/8	7 5/8	6 7/8	8	8	Sonoma county, CA	Christian Weise	1851	2
341 4/8	49 5/8	52 2/8	48 3/8	7 6/8	7 5/8	8	7	solano County, CA	Alvin M. Wallen	1990	3
336 7/8	49 2/8	48 6/8	45 2/8	7 5/8	7 5/8	8	8	San Luis Obispo County, CA	Pick up	1996	4
332 4/8	52 2/8	51 6/8	40 2/8	10 1/8	10 5/8	8	7	Del Norte county, CA	Jim Schaafsma	1996	5
330 1/8	52 3/8	52 4/8	38 4/8	7 6/8	7 2/8	9	7	Solano county, CA	Tod L. Reichert	1999	6
319 2/8	47 6/8	43	44 7/8	6 6/8	7 4/8	8	7	Solano County, CA	H. James Tonkins, Jr.	1992	7
317 3/8	51 5/8	49 6/8	39 4/8	7 4/8	7 4/8	9	8	Solano County, CA	Donald L. Potter	1996	8
315 4/8	46 4/8	48 7/8	39 7/8	7 6/8	7 2/8	7	7	Solano County, CA	David G. Poullin	1994	9
309 2/8	44 7/8	43 5/8	47 1/8	10 2/8	9 7/8	10	9	Solano County, CA	Stan Atwood	2000	10
308 6/8	10 4/8	42 4/8	52	8 1/8	8 1/8	8	6	San Luis Obispo County, CA	Ray M. Tonkin	1999	11
296 1/8	45 3/8	44 2/8	41	7	7 1/8	6	7	Monterey County, CA	Norman Fre	1997	12
283 5/8	36	35 6/8	35 3/8	8 2/8	8 4/8	7	7	San Luis Obispo County, CA	Pamela Atwood	1996	13
277	42 5/8	42 5/8	40 7/8	8	8	6	7	Mendocino County, CA	Scott L. Brothers	1995	14
273 6/8	38 6/8	38 4/8	34 1/8	7 4/8	7 3/8	7	7	Monterey County, CA	Harry Marx	1991	15
273 4/8	37	43 6/8	42	7 2/8	7 3/8	7	7	San Luis Obispo County, CA	Rex Baker	2000	16
266 3/8	44 5/8	43 3/8	43 2/8	7 3/8	6 6/8	7	8	Monterey County, CA	Casey Brooks	2000	17
265 5/8	37 5/8	37 2/8	39	4 6/8	5	7	7	Monterey County, CA	Carelton Nordschow	1997	18
259	39	39	43	6 2/8	6 1/8	6	6	Monterey County, CA	Harry Marx	1993	19
248 6/8	37 1/8	38 3/8	31 1/8	6 6/8	6 6/8	6	6	Lone Pine, CA	Stan Atwood	1991	20
403*	45 6/8	43 1/8	37 6/8	10 3/8	9 5/8	10	12	Solano County, CA	Pick up	1995	
365*	48	47 3/8	41 3/8	8 4/8	8 6/8	9	8	Solano County, CA	Bryce Evans	1997	
324 6/8*	43 6/8	44 2/8	40 4/8	8 4/8	8 1/8	10	9	Solano County, CA	David Newsom	1991	
311 4/8*	41 5/8	40 4/8	38 3/8	8 7/8	7 7/8	10	10	Solano County, CA	Paul Osmond	1999	

*Final Score subject to revision by additional verifying measurements

Grizzly Island
Solano County
Photos courtesy of Richard Cox

California hunter Jim Tonkin with his trophy tule elk.

The Governor's Tag
Tule Elk Hunt

Reprinted from California Hunter December/January 1993

"I see his orange vest," someone announces.

"I see him too, " echoes another. "He's directly in line with the first of the three smokestacks way in the background."

Finally, I saw him. Even with 10X binoculars it was difficult to find the small orange dot at that great of a distance. The hot August afternoon sun was not helping as it produced some heat waves which made our viewing even more difficult. We estimated that the hunter was 1200 to 1500 yards away from us.

Once more I lost sight of him as he went into a crawl heading in the direction of the elk.

I quickly moved the binoculars to the right to see if the tule elk were still in the same location. They apparently had not seen the hunter and continued their afternoon rest. Occasionally a few would stand and then lie back down. Unless they were standing, we could only see the tops of some antlers from our vantage point. We couldn't tell how many elk made up the group and the distance made the terrain deceptive. The only thing we knew was that one of Grizzly Island Wildlife Area's largest tule elk bulls was supposed to be in that location.

What was to have been just a quick trip to view some tule elk from the vantage point of a Fish and Game maintenance building had now turned into a three-hour-plus, eye-squinting, sun-baking, long-distance view of a hunter's stalk for a trophy bull.

I was with Department of Fish and Game employees and also members of the Sacramento Safari Club. All were playing supporting roles in the 1992 Governor's Tag Tule Elk Hunt.

The wind was blowing like it does most of the time in the hills and marshes west of Fairfield, but today it was not cooling the hot August afternoon.

Suddenly a large herd of elk jumped to their feet and began to run to the north. Because of the wind we could not tell if a shot had been fired. The herd had not run far before they slowed to a walk and continued to move north.

"There's Tonkin," someone said.

The hunter was now standing and looking in the direction the elk were headed. We all began asking questions. "Had he spooked the elk?" "Wasn't the one he was looking for there?" "Did he shoot and miss?" We were just too far away to tell.

It had been two days earlier when I had driven onto the Grizzly Island Wildlife Area for the first time in over twelve years. Time had made me forget that the 10-mile drive in from Fairfield to the wildlife area was on a winding two-lane road which added more to my travel time than I had planned.

I was trying to arrive for the orientation meeting which was being held that evening, before the elk hunt. As I pulled up to the camp, the meeting was just finishing.

I was surprised at what I saw. There were a number of camp trailers, tents and a large canvas cook tent set up in a grove of eucalyptus trees. As I entered the camp I met Ed Nanini, past president of the Sacramento Safari Club. Ed introduced me to the two successful bidders for this year's hunt – Jim Tonkin of Morgan Hill and Jim Hatcher of Bend, Oregon. Tonkin had been the high bidder at $20,000 at the February 1992 Sacramento Safari Club's 13th Annual Auction and Jim Hatcher had bid $22,000 at the Rocky Mountain Elk Foundation Convention.

Accompanying Tonkin was his wife Sheryll. Hatcher had brought his daughter, Sharon Hatcher, to share the excitement with him. Both ladies are experienced hunters and were looking forward to the hunts.

The Sacramento Safari Club and the Rocky Mountain Elk Foundation had members in camp to help with anything that needed to be done. The excitement level in the camp was so high you would have thought that everyone had an elk tag.

Hatcher was shooting a .300 Winchester Magnum, and Tonkin was using a .375/.284 JDJ pistol. The pistol was capable of sending its 250-grain Sierra bullet 2000 feet per second.

Tonkin had taken game with a rifle and archery equipment in the past. Lately the pistol had become his weapon of choice.

A hunter since he was 12-years-old, Tonkin and an acquaintance had scouted the tule elk for the past three weeks. He had picked the one bull he wanted from the herd of approximately 140 elk. He was prepared to spend the entire 30 day season to get that bull.

According to Dennis Becker, wild-life habitat supervisor at Grizzly Island, each hunter is allowed to have one person accompany them into the field on the hunt. In addition, they are restricted to hunting only on the wild-life area. If the elk are chased off onto adjacent private property, the hunters cannot pursue them.

On opening morning the two hunters left in separate vehicles with their hunting companions. All of the others involved stayed in camp waiting for word. Around noon both hunters returned. They each told of the numerous cows and bulls they had seen.

Hatcher had passed on a number of bulls, waiting to spot a larger one.

Tonkin, on the other had, had spotted his bull with three others, and after a short stalk had positioned himself for a shot. He was shocked when he pulled the trigger and his pistol gave off the sound of a weak .22. His reload had misfired, sending the bullet far short of its intended target. The elk moved out of range and while Tonkin attempted to get into a position for another shot, the elk crossed a river and moved onto private property.

"That's the one I want. I'll wait until he comes back," said Tonkin.

Late in the afternoon both hunters again took to the hunting area, glassing for bulls. Again we waited in camp for word of success.

It was around 5:00 p.m. when word reached camp via DFG personnel that Hatcher had taken a bull. Everyone had smiles on their faces as we grabbed our cameras and headed for the vehicles.

Jon Fischer, the elk program coordinator for the Department of Fish and Game, wanted to weigh the animal before it was field dressed. That was going to take a number of us to help load the animal on a trailer so it could be taken to a scale located at camp.

When we reached Hatcher, he had a smile which told me this hunt was well worth it.

Hatcher explained that from a distance of about 1000 yards they had been glassing a herd which had a large bull and many cows. Another bull, which apparently had moved into the wildlife area from private property that afternoon, had suddenly started moving in the direction of the herd they were watching. Before it got to the herd it had stopped, reversed directions and then had lain down.

For at least 10 minutes they studied the racks of both bulls, trying to determine which one would score higher. Finally it was decided that the resting bull had the larger set of antlers.

A large mound approximately 100 yards from the resting bull provided the cover needed to close the distance between Hatcher and the bull. After he had reached the mound, the bull stood up. A well-placed shot behind the front shoulder proved fatal as the bull took just a couple of steps before collapsing.

The bull weighted 790 pounds and its rack scored 315 points.

The camp that evening was like most hunting camps. Everyone was happy because of Hatcher's success that day and the hunt was retold many times.

Also during the evening much speculation was done regarding whether the bull Tonkin was after would move back into the wildlife area that night.

On the second day of the hunt, Tonkin was out early to find his bull. He returned late in the morning to tell everyone that he had spotted the bull in the hunting area but it was too close to private property. He did not want to take a chance on spooking it out again, so he was going to give it a chance to bed down and then try a stalk.

A spotting run by Tonkin around noon produced the location of the bull. It was shortly after that when he decided to make the stalk. We all wished him well as he drove off.

Wanting to get an idea of the challenge facing Tonkin, some of us drove to the DFG maintenance area mentioned earlier.

Now as we tried to figure out what was happening by Tonkin's hand signals some 1200 yards away, Fish and Game personnel radioed that Tonkin's bull was down.

Once more we raced to the hunter's location – this time to congratulate Tonkin, take some memorable photographs, and help with the elk.

As everyone gathered around the elk, Tonkin told me about the three-hour stalk that I had only been able to partially observe.

He had driven south on a road that took them past the area where the elk were bedded. He wanted to stalk the animals coming from the south as the north wind would be in his face. That way if the animals spooked, they would most likely stay within the wildlife area. When he began his stalk he was about 1500 yards from the herd. The weeds, grasses, and levees afforded concealment for most of the stalk.

The herd was lying in a large depression mostly devoid of any vegetation. Approximately 360 yards from the herd he was forced to crawl on his hands and knees to keep out of sight. He did this for about 200 yards. At this point no other cover existed. Now 157 yards away, there was his bull lying in the center of a group of 26 other bulls.

Tonkin had stopped his advance behind the last bush which could provide cover. Using his daypack as a rest, he positioned himself for a shot at the bull. With other animals behind the one he wanted, he was forced to wait for the bull to stand. More than 30 minutes passed as Tonkin watched the herd. Suddenly the moment came as his bull stood up. With crosshairs behind the front shoulder, he squeezed the trigger. The bull turned quartering toward Tonkin – an instant later its legs buckled and the bull dropped in its tracks. The bullet had pierced its heart as it passed through the bull.

Tonkin had just taken the first tule elk with a pistol. It currently is expected to rank in 6th place with a score of 326 2/8. The elk weighed 785 pounds on the Grizzly Island scale and filled his freezer with 480 pounds of wrapped meat.

While both hunters provided hunts that will be forever remembered, what is even more important is their financial contribution to the future of both the California tule elk, and for hunting and hunters in California.

Tule Elk taken by Ray Tonkin in 1999
with Twisselman Outfitters
305 net B&C

Tule Elk taken on Grizzly Island in 1999. 9 x 7 330 1/8 net B&C
Left: Hunting Editor for Outdoor Life Magazine, Jim Zumbo
Center: Hunter, Todd Reichert

World Record "Muzzle Loader" Tule Elk
1998 Grizzly Island 325 ⁵/₈ net B&C
Left: Hunter, Robert Keenan   Right: Guide, Richard Cox

ROCKY MOUNTAIN ELK

Non-Typical Rocky Mountain Elk
Number One
Score: 420 4/8
Location: Tejon Ranch, Kern County
Date: 2000

ROCKY MOUNTAIN ELK - NON-TYPICAL

Cervus Elaphus

Score	Length of Main Beam		Inside Spread	Circumference at smallest place between first & second points		Number of Points		Locality	Hunter	Date Killed	Rank
	Right	Left		Right	Left	Right	Left				

Minimum Score 385

Score	Right	Left	Spread	Right	Left	Right	Left	Locality	Hunter	Date Killed	Rank
420 4/8	52	55 5/8	36 2/8	10 4/8	10 4/8	8	9	KERN COUNTY, CA	BRAD PETERS	2000	1

ROOSEVELT ELK

Roosevelt Elk
Number One
Score: 371⁵/₈
Location: Smith River Humbolt Co.
Date: 2000
Hunter: Robert H. Gaynor

Roosevelt Elk
Number Two
Score: 343 ²/₈
Location: Humbolt County
Date: 1992
Hunter: Pick Up
Owner: Gary Backanen

Roosevelt Elk
Number Three
Score: 338 7/8
Location: Big Lagoon, Humbolt County
Date: 2000
Hunter: Paul E. Benoit

Big Lagoon Elk Hunt

Humbolt County, California
By Paul Benoit, San Juan Bautista, California

Last May I applied for a Roosevelt Elk tag for the Big Lagoon Hunt in Humbolt County. I was notified after the drawing in Sacramento that I had been the 17th application picked out of the 25 tags issued. The hunt was scheduled to start on Wednesday, August 30th and last 10 days, ending September 8th, 2000. This was an either sex hunt – spikes included.

There was a mandatory orientation held on Tuesday before the hunt at the Simpson Lumber Headquarters at Big Lagoon. During the orientation 25 anxious elk hunters learned that we would be hunting on 70,000 acres of Simpson Land with more than 1500 miles of roads.

Karen Kovac from CDF&G out of the Eureka office was the chairperson for the orientation. Warden Wilcox covered the game laws and safety concerns for the hunt. These wardens explained what hunting conditions to expect and what fish & game expected in return from every hunter (tissue & stool sample, tooth).

Tom McDonald of Simpson Timber Company addressed the hunters explaining what logging areas were out of bounds. The rules for checking in and out each day of the hunt and the boundaries of Simpson Timber. Detailed maps were available for $10.00 and virtually every hunter bought one. After the orientation meeting every hunter was allowed to drive around and familiarize him/herself with the hunt area.

Big Lagoon was unlike any other Elk hunt I have been on in Wyoming or Colorado. It was a little overwhelming driving the roads, some came to dead ends and with virtually little visibility with so much vegetation and trees no one saw an elk after scouting the area. The timber is so dense binoculars and spotting scopes remained in the truck. There is so much feed and water these elk are not forced to move much to be very content. The elk had not started to rut so bugleing was a waste of time. The hunting area is extremely rugged and heavy timber limits any long shooting you might encounter on an out of state hunt. Each hunter was allowed two people to help during the hunt and one gun only per hunter was allowed. My best friend and girlfriend, Sandy Williams, along with my daughter, Sarah Jane Benoit accompanied me on the hunt. Sarah only stayed the first 2 days before she returned to her home in Cedarville.

Sandy and myself hunted religiously 7 days, driving roads and walking before I even saw any elk in the hunt area. On the 8th day of the hunt, after being directed on our map to one area by one hunter there was not even a sign – it was pretty discouraging. After taking a break we drove to hunt a new area in the southern portion of the hunt area known as the M-Line. By then it was late in the afternoon. After parking the truck we decided to hike along an old abandoned logging road. Walking quietly for about a half mile we started finding some encouraging signs. Trees with fresh scrapes, wallow, and fresh droppings. We were both excited after pounding the ground for eight days. As we rounded a turn in the road we walked up on some cows and raghorns feeding in a draw above us. The wind was traveling upslope and immediately the elk bolted back along the sidehill moving parallel with the logging road and the ridgeline of the mountain.

I told my partner to walk slowly down the road back toward the truck and I hustled up to the ridgetop about 550 yards. The wind was blowing straight up the mountain so I knew the elk couldn't wind me, but they would surely wind my partner down below them. I hoped it would be enough to hold the elk in the timber as there were lots of elk beds, this was where these elk were living.

I slowly worked my way along the ridge working down and then back up only to move farther down the top of the ridge to repeat the same track. The seventh time I worked my way into the timber I saw the bull standing on an old skid trail about 120 yards down the mountain. He was looking down toward the rest of his herd and I believe he was winding Sandy who was 700 yards below him. The bull never knew I was above him and I shot him in the neck once as the head and neck were the only part of the elk I could see clearly. It all happened very fast. The frustration and anxiety finally paid off with a 7 & 7 pt. bull.

I marked the trail down to the logging road to get my partner so we could start the work. She hiked over the mountain to the opposite side to see if there was a more accessible road, as this was going to be quite a chore with just the two of us and no communicable access to help. While I field dressed the bull, she flagged the road on the other side of the ridge. While she stayed with the bull, I drove around the mountain, it took about a half hour, I found her flagging and locked the hubs, I was able to work the truck down to the bull by using an abandoned skid trail. After I got the truck below the bull we loaded the bull with a come-a-long bridled around the headboard of the truck.

We skinned the bull out by flashlight slowly hoisting the bull from the bed of my old Ford diesel truck, using the same come-a-long. We called from Big Lagoon, Gene Maretin in McKinleyville and reached his locker about 10:30 pm where we quartered and hung the meat. Returning to camp about 12:30 we were very tired but very happy, what a great hunt.

I met some very nice people on this hunt. Simpson Timber at Big Lagoon certainly has the best elk hunt in California as there were many bulls in the 300 plus class killed. Tom McDonald and all the employees of Simpson Timber Co. were extremely helpful to all the hunters. Tom McDonald himself worked with the hunters to retrieve at least 15 elk that were killed during the hunt. They were exceptionally gracious hosts, this was much appreciated by all the hunters.

This was an elk hunt I will have great memories for a lifetime.

Roosevelt Elk
Number Four
Score: 337 5/8
Location: Humbolt County
Date: 1992
Hunter: Gary Backanen

ROOSEVELT'S ELK
Cervus Elaphus Roosevelti

Score	Length of Main Beam		Inside Spread	Circumference at smallest place between first & second points		Number of Points		Locality	Hunter	Date Killed	Rank
	Right	Left		Right	Left	Right	Left				
371 5/8	53 4/8	55 4/8	37 3/8	8 6/8	8 2/8	8	8	Smith River, CA	Robert H. Gaynor	2000	1
343 2/8	55	56 4/8	34 3/8	7 2/8	7 4/8	6	7	Humboldt County, CA	Pick up	1992	2
338 7/8	49 6/8	50 4/8	43	8	7 4/8	7	7	Big Lagoon, CA	Paul E. Benoit	2000	3
337 5/8	57 5/8	53 2/8	33 2/8	7 2/8	7 5/8	8	8	Humboldt County, CA	Pick up	1992	4
332 4/8	52 2/8	51 6/8	40 2/8	10 1/8	10 5/8	8	7	Del Norte County, CA	Jim Schaafsma	1996	5
332 2/8	51 6/8	51 4/8	41 2/8	8 6/8	9 1/8	8	6	Humboldt County, CA	Pick up	1955	6
330 5/8	53 2/8	55 1/8	38 2/8	7 1/8	7 7/8	6	6	Siskiyou County, CA	William D. Johnson	1997	7
327	49 4/8	50 5/8	38 4/8	9 4/8	9 7/8	6	6	Del Norte County, CA	Patrick J. Papsergia	1996	8
325 1/8	52 4/8	51	39 1/8	9 1/8	8 2/8	6	6	Siskiyou County, CA	Jeremy W. Johnson	1997	9
318 5/8	48	49 2/8	40	8 2/8	8	7	6	Del Norte County, CA	Richard K. Armas	1988	10
307 2/8	48 1/8	45 7/8	39 7/8	9 1/8	8 2/8	7	7	Siskiyou County, CA	Bill Kleaver	1997	11
306 4/8	47	47 5/8	43 5/8	7 5/8	7 6/8	6	6	Humboldt County, CA	Michael L. Johnson	1976	12
300 1/8	47 3/8	48 6/8	34	8 3/8	8 4/8	6	6	Del Norte County, CA	Paul Kunzler	1999	13
299	47 6/8	46 2/8	33 3/8	8 6/8	7 7/8	7	6	Del Norte County, CA	Glenn W. Ng	2000	14
298 2/8	47 6/8	47 2/8	40 5/8	9	9	6	6	Humboldt County, CA	Eugene M. Boyd IV	1988	15
297 5/8	45 6/8	44 6/8	39 7/8	8 3/8	8 1/8	6	6	Del Norte County, CA	Ronald F. Cibart	2000	16
297 4/8	48 1/8	45 4/8	40 5/8	7 4/8	7 6/8	6	6	Siskiyou County, CA	Michael R. Bell	1996	17

Photos and Short Stories

Ben Nuckolls, Animal Control officer for El Dorado County, sent in some photos. Above is a road kill buck from Placerville. Below is a buck stuck in a fence on American River Parkway, Sacramento.

This picture was sent to me by Chris Lacey of Reno, Nevada. The buck was shot out of season near Eagleville. The antlers were acquired from the Fish and Game by a butcher in Cederville when the meat was brought in by the wardens to be processed. Chris, who is a Boone & Crockett scorer, taped this monarch a 258 points net B & C

Austin Saunders, stepson of Scott Wilkinson took this buck in Zone A in the 2000 season.

Richard Chagolla took this fine mule deer cross in Ventura County, Zone D13. The buck scored 160 6/8 and sported a 27" spread.

Scott Wilkinson and Greg Milloway shared a successful muzzleloader hunt in northeast California. The upper buck is a 26" 6 x 4 taken by Scott while the buck in the lower photo was taken by Greg and has a 29 7/8" spread.

Bill Jarrell took this fine blacktail buck west of Yreka in Siskiyou County in 1997. it officially scored 144 6/8 B&C

Art Tong, of Truckee, California harvested this fine buck back in 1981 in Zone D-5 near the El Dorado Hills. The buck sports a 28 1/2" outside spread.

Greg Milloway shot this huge 4 x 4 blacktail during the 1997 A zone season in Monterey County.

Scott Wilkinson harvested this blacktail buck in West Stanislaus County during the 1998 A zone season. The buck dressed out at 161 lbs. and had a Boone & Crockett score of 152 5/8 net. Pictured are left to right Bob White and Scott Wilkinson.

This blacktail buck was taken by Robert Fellom in 1997 from Santa Clara County. The buck scores 150 6/8 Boone & Crockett.

Ray Douglas's 267 4/8 point buck from Mariposa County 1948.

This mule deer was taken by an 80 year old hunter in Modoc County back in 1980. It has 30 scorable points and about a 35" spread. The owner of the store would not let us take it off the wall to score the antlers, but it surely would make the Boone & Crockett minimum for the non-typical category.

This head is known as the Tennant Buck, taken from Tennant, California by Major Thomas in 1916. It is 40" wide with 29 points and scores approximately 271 Boone & Crockett points. A cracked skull plate keeps it out of the record books.

This non-typical mule deer originally appeared in the third edition of the Nevada Wildlife Record book. The picture was acquired by their committee with the caption that read, Elko County, Nevada.

Actually this buck was taken years ago in Modoc County, California by the famous taxidermist, Al Hilbert, from Sacramento, California. The head disappeared after his death and is long sought after by the California Deer Association Wildlife Record Book Committee.

This giant forked horn was taken by Charles Stone back in 1922 from Calavaras County. The buck has a 31" outside spread and 29" main beams. The antlers score an impressive 145 net Boone & Crockett points.

This buck was harvested by Don Stemler in Calavaras County back in 1976. It is a 9 x 10 with a 30 5/8" outside spread and scoring 203 1/8 net Boone & Crockett points.

These bucks were taken by Babe Stone in Calavaras County.

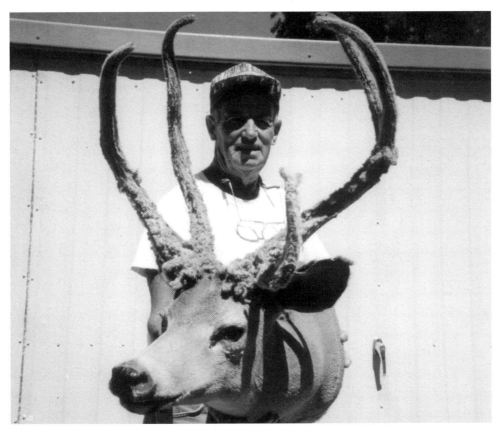

These bucks were taken by Babe Stone in Calavaras County.

These bucks were taken by Babe Stone's brother, Walt Stone in Calavaras County. Both of these bucks are over 30" wide.

The top buck was taken by Walt Stone's son in Calavaras County. The buck stretches the tape to over 28" wide. The lower photo is of a buck taken by Cody Stemler's grandfather, Don Stemler. He harvested the big mule deer in Modoc County back in 1939. The antlers score an even 187 net Boone & Crockett.

This outstanding buck was taken by Walter Valente in Calavaras County back in 1945. Walter had spotted the buck while checking cattle on horseback. There were six bucks around a cattle salt lick but this one was unlike any Walter had ever seen. Walter said, "the big non-typical had the most blue velvet on his antlers." Walter rode his horse into the trees, so not to spook the bucks, and there he watched them as they worked their way up onto a steep brushy side hill to bed for the day.

Opening day he took relatives to the exact location to form a drive. Walter positioned himself where he thought the bucks would exit. Everything worked out perfect and the big buck came right up the mountain jumping boulders and brush right to him. One shot and the buck was his. The antlers are 33 1/2" wide with 27 scorable points. With a score of 232 1/8 Boone and Crockett points it puts the buck up amongst the top heads ever taken in California.

Pictured is Walter Valente, Sr. left and Walter's son Walt on the right.

Front and rear view of Walter Valente's fine non-typical buck. Pictured is Cody Stemler holding the buck.

Side pictures of Walter Valente's big buck.

This massive buck was taken by Joel Sakamoto near his home in Morgan Hill. The 4 x 3 has a 24 1/2" spread and scores over 135 Boone & Crockett points.

This buck was taken by Tim Koester, Jr. in Monterey County during the 2001 season. The antlers measure 24 1/2" wide and have five eye guardes on the right and four on the left.

This huge 4 x 4 was taken by Jeff Masselli in the Sierra foothills during the D-5 season.

The Nelson Buck

Don Nelson's thirty-two year quest for a record book mule deer finally came to an end in the year 2000. He discovered he had it all along!

By Ken Nelson

Don Nelson and Bob White were hunting and fishing partners, as well as co-workers, when they were looking over the 1968 California hunting regulations. They commonly hunted the coastal foothills for the diminutive blacktail deer. When they saw a special controlled hunt scheduled for late November and early December in Mariposa County, they knew right away that their chances at a big buck would be excellent. A limited number of doe tags were offered in the drawing, as well as a handful of either-sex tags. They applied for either-sex tags knowing that their chances of being drawn were slim to none. Needles to say, when they were notified that they had been successful in the drawing, they were ecstatic.

In planning their hunt, Don and Bob decided to hunt the extremely rugged Merced River canyon at the end of the season. They reasoned that the rut would be in full swing, and that deer would be migrating out of the high country from Yosemite National Park. A migration hunt in the rut would be their dream come true!

On December 7th they checked into a motel in the town of El Portal. They asked the manager about deer hunting in the area, and the man told them there were plenty of does on the national forest lands surrounding the town. Don and Bob advised him that they had drawn either-sex tags, and they were not interested in hunting for does. "Bucks!

You guys are hunting bucks?" The manager sounded like he was getting buck fever. He excitedly explained directions to an area he knew of where large bucks from Yosemite commonly wintered after being driven from the park by heavy snows. He had seen them there in the past, after the close of the general deer season. There was heavy snow in the park at the time, and the hunting area outside the park was free of snow. "There will be nice bucks there," the manager said with confidence.

At first light, Don Nelson and Bob White arrived at the hunting area described by the manager of the motel. From their vantage point along the Merced River, they could not see to the top of the ridge above. They started hiking up the extremely steep and rocky slope. After 3 1/2 hours of sweaty climbing they were getting exhausted and still had not reached the top. The terrain was getting even steeper and it was starting to look like mountain goat habitat. Don found a game trail that went side hill. He decided to follow the trail while Bob went side hill about 100 yards above Don. They were hunting at an elevation between 3500 and 4000 feet when Don Nelson jumped the huge non-typical from his bed at about 10:00 a.m. The buck took off out of a small patch of manzanita brush at close range. Don watched with his mouth open as the buck disappeared around a hog back ridge. He explained that he could not believe the size of the buck he had just seen. He had momentarily forgotten that he was supposed to be deer hunting. When Don came to his senses a second later, he ran for the hog back which the buck had disappeared around. As he crested the ridge he saw the buck stop trotting and look back. From a distance of 50 to 60 yards Don could see only the head and neck of the buck over the top of a brush patch. Don lifted his Remington pump action .270 and put the cross hairs of the 4X Leupold scope on the bucks neck,. At the shot, the buck was down. The 130 grain Nosler Partition bullet had done it's job. That's when the buck fever hit.

"Did you get him?" Bob called out from above.

"I got him!" Don replied.

"How many points?"

"I don't know. He's got points all over his head!" Don looked down and he could see the Merced River far below.

Bob hiked down to Don's location where they field dressed the buck. Bob wanted to pack it out then, but Don persuaded him to keep hunting due to the difficult time they had just getting to the hunting area. They agreed to pack out the buck after Bob had a chance to find a buck.

It did not take long. Bob took a long cross-canyon shot at a nice 4 x 4 but was unable to connect. Then Don and Bob spotted a big buck that had orange surveyor's tape tied to it's antlers. They did not know what to make of that, so Bob did not shoot. Finally, an hour and a half after Don had killed his trophy, the two hunters spotted a very heavy antlered 5 x 4 point buck with a 25 inch spread. Bob nailed him with his .270, and their hunt was over. Two trophy bucks in one day!

Now everybody knew that Don Nelson had taken one monster buck. The taxidermist said it was the biggest buck he had ever seen taken in California. But Don is a modest man who was content to have the buck on the wall of his trophy room. A man from a sportsman's group came over to the house to look at it one day, but he said the main frame was too small, and it would not make The Book. So for thirty plus years, Don would tell people, "Yes he's big, but he doesn't quite make The Book."

Since my father, Don, is getting along in age now, and the chances are remote of him (or me) getting a larger buck, I took the head off the wall one day and took some measurements. "I think this buck will make the Boone and Crockett book," I told him. My brother, Mike Nelson, had taken a Boone and Crockett mule deer in Idaho the prior year, and I touched on the right words to prod him along into getting the buck officially scored when I told him, "This buck is bigger than Mike's."

That's all it took. Don took the head to an official Boone and Crockett measurer who added up an official score of 244 2/8. The 14 x 12 point rack is from one of the biggest bucks ever taken in California.